MIDDLESEX VOL II

Edited by Claire Tupholme

First published in Great Britain in 2003 by
YOUNG WRITERS
Remus House,
Coltsfoot Drive,
Peterborough, PE2 9JX
Telephone (01733) 890066

HB ISBN 0 75434 325 1
SB ISBN 0 75434 326 X

FOREWORD

This year, the Young Writers' The Write Stuff! competition proudly presents a showcase of the best poetic talent from over 40,000 up-and-coming writers nationwide.

Young Writers was established in 1991 and we are still successful, even in today's modern world, in promoting and encouraging the reading and writing of poetry.

The thought, effort, imagination and hard work put into each poem impressed us all, and once again, the task of selecting poems was a difficult one, but nevertheless, an enjoyable experience.

We hope you are as pleased as we are with the final selection and that you and your family continue to be entertained with *The Write Stuff! Middlesex Vol II* for many years to come.

CONTENTS

Nishma Malde	53
Mishri Amin	53
Melanie Dhanaratne	54
Mehreen H Kassam	54
Douriya Jodiyawalla	55
Leila Chawla	55
Dami Sunmonu	56
Leena Patel	56
Isabelle Tranter	57
Zara Chung	57
Roxanna Baker	58
Sharmili Balarajah	58
Janki Rabheru	59
Carmen Liu	60
Sarrumathy Sivanesan	61
Clare Moore	62
Shalina Patel	62
Sandani Chandrasekara	63
Rushani Selvendran	64
Aziza Phillips	64
Lindsay Phillips	65
Jessica Agius	65
Bhavnisha Modi	66
Bethany Wellington	66
Nicola Allen	67
Sarah Turner	68
Thivya Sritharan	69
Ayia Abbas	70
Sarah Browne	71
Annika Dattani	72

Orleans Park School

Sammy Letham	72
Emma Deacon	73
Safiyya Hussein	73
Eleanor Massey	74
Charlotte Cushen	75
Sophie Deacon	76

Sophie De Frond 76
Alex McKenna 77
Grace Rake 77
Stephanos Koutroumanidis 78
Chelsea Brown 78
Sam Riedlinger 79
George Barnes 80
Ami Kitch 80
Emma Hastings 81
Ben King 81
Roxanne Bates 82
Jamie Atkins 82
Chandni Babbar 83
Matthew Brandon 83
Eleanor Batson 84
Melissa Patel 84
Marina Hutchins Garcia 85
Alex Juriansz 85
Liam Cooper-King 86
Ashley Rollins 87
Hanna Clarke 88
Ewan Henry 88
Steven Winter 89
Michael Hughes 90
Ivan Woloshak 90
Geraint Thomas 91
Eleanor Thompson 91
Jessica Cole 92
Lily Beck 92
Jodie McKnight 93
Katherine Underhill 94
Massimo Galletia 94
Jamie Elliott 95
Luan Austin-Duch 95

Preston Manor High School
Sabina Akhtar 96
David Ahn 97

Reanne Sinclair	98
Christopher Sedze	98
Kinari Mehta	99
Samir	99
Sabina Akhtar	100
Harkaran Bajwa	101
Teresa Hays	102
Bhavesh Patel	102
Dwayne Omaghomi	103
Stephanie	103
Sarah Hamoudi	104
Jason Ellis Condison	105
Shikha Karki	106
Rajan Aurora	106
Davinia Champaneri	107
Sarah Hamoudi	108
Sana Rasoul	108
Ayesha Patel	109
Arti Bhundia	109
Paul Fergus	110
Mostafa Mohammed-Ali	110
Manisha P Bhudia	111
Nigel Ngo	112
Jason Condison	113
Fahd Saleem	114
Ehsan Salehi	115
Mostafa Mohammed-Ali	116

St Catherine's School, Twickenham

Binal Patel	117
Nadine Rajan	118
Tamsin Austin	119
Bajel Patel	120
Carly Byrne	120
Lisa Widger	121
Rochelle Mayner	122
Yasmin Raza	122
Imogen West	123

The Poems

FALLING

Endless days and weeks pass by,
How hard it seems to like this life.
Time unchained, prolongs an eternal strife
Yet it begrudges how little they tried.

Plight and despair fill an endless void,
Hope once lived, never again
For that land and people long forsaken,
A world apart and with storms, torn.

Dust and smoke among fractured earth,
Fields of hate withered away,
Death, summoned, has come this way,
In deep emotion they drove a plague.

What remains? That has not yet passed,
Little fact will debris yield
For once a great war, relentless, raged,
Its tale few now live to say.

Weapons they bore, naked to the eye,
Unimaginable power, to clear a world,
Yet the Earth cares not
Its troubles had long passed.

The age of men, once held proud
Had withered the world, at present dawn
Relieved of pain, the Earth sighed,
For men doomed themselves, none tried.

Chan Sivanesan (16)

WAR, WHAT IS IT GOOD FOR?

War is pointless, no more war.
War, what is it good for?
Planes, bombs, tanks and mortars
All used to kill our sons and daughters.

Billions spent on rockets and bombs.
Children's hospitals starved of funds.
Fire a missile, a million dollars,
Better spent on schools and scholars.

Scared and homeless, nowhere to flee,
No food to feed the refugees.
Lots of wars in many places,
Still the same terror on their faces.

We must control this need to fight
And urge all governments to get it right,
To negotiate till the thirteenth hour,
Not sort it out with military power.

I'm only twelve, not in my teens,
Taliban, Chechen and Mujahden.
I've heard of all of these and many more,
I ask again, war, what is it good for?

Brooke Day (12)
Heathfield School

RUN, RUN, RUN!

Standing there in the rain,
People must think that we're insane.
Here the ball comes,
I scoop it up and
Run, run, run!

Shooting sharply,
Flying ball.
I look up at the players,
They are so shockingly tall!
Sam passes the ball
And yes I catch it and
Run, run, run!

Zara Wilkinson (11)
Heathfield School

ANIMALS

The child looking around, searching
Without giving up,
Not knowing it's gone,
Gone forever,
Never coming back . . .
Calling out for his mum for help
With no clue where to search,
Where to go
Or where to find her and where he lived.

Puzzled and clueless
Going around in circles,
Time goes by
And finally he can recognise the smell
And puts on a happy face,
But it looks different,
No trees, no grass, nothing,
Nothing except creatures he has never seen before
Roaming about in his homeland,
Then he realises
He's facing the real world . . .

Mina Nishimura (13)
Heathfield School

WHY?

Jenny was a stupid girl,
She couldn't even do a twirl.
She always said she didn't care,
She couldn't even carry out a dare.

No one in her class, 10K liked her,
She was selected as the captain of litter.
They always treated her mean
And sometimes they acted like she wasn't to be seen.

Class 10K once played a prank,
The plan was cool but oh it stank.
They filled her sandwiches with raw fish
But Jenny was allergic and she came out with an itch.

Going back to school she thought everyone would worry
But no one even said sorry.
The girls in the class were the same as before,
They took pleasure in the fear and they wanted to see more.

She couldn't take any more
So decided to go to a large cliff she had seen the day before.
I leave you this letter 10K which states the reason
Why I jumped off this cliff at the end of the season.

Kapila Rudra (12)
Heathfield School

SILENCE

The slug slithers and slimes when it rains,
The thumping of the blue tit's wings as it flies,
The geckos swiftly running through the rocks
And the sound of the sand being crushed under your feet.

Aisha Turner (11)
Heathfield School

ROAD TO FREEDOM

Creeping along the passageway
She hoped not to be caught.

Even a whisper
Made her heart thump out.

Jailed by her kidnappers,
Being forced to escape.

A dog barked a warning,
She sprinted away.

Every sound scared her,
She needed company.

Lonely and in solitude,
Hoping not to be caught again.

How would she escape?
She was still in the dark.

She carried on running to see the light,
Hoping to reach it one day.

Aparna Shankar (13)
Heathfield School

SILENCE

Silence is when you can hear things listen:
The delicate clicking of a money spider as it runs down the bath;
The rustle of a blue tit as it shakes its feathers in the wind;
The soft slurp of a lizard's tongue as it catches its prey;
And the delicate dripping of the morning dew on the grass.

Chelsea Milsom (12)
Heathfield School

AT SCHOOL

I walk into an enormous school
With huge windows and a great playing field,
I give myself a tour of the school,
The sports hall, the main hall and all the spacious classrooms.

The teachers are generally great fun,
But we do have some boring ones,
I get out my pens and pencils
And get started with my work.

At lunch the food is *yucky!*
Lumpy mash potato and smelly vegetables,
The soapy cups are horrible
And the cutlery is even worse.

At last, the end of school has come,
But now I'm waiting for the school coach to arrive.
The seats on the coach are uncomfortable
And the air conditioning doesn't work.

Now I've got to wait for another exciting day at school
To see all my friends again
And to do tons of work.

Jessica Chamberlain (12)
Heathfield School

MY GERBILS

Sugar and Spice are two of my delights,
When I go in the room they tend to take flight,
In their cage there are toys you see,
They get their food by coming up to me,
They run up and down squeaking happily as they run,
They crawl over and under, they think it's excellent fun.

Sometimes I go in and they come and say hello,
When you say some sort of word like hi or go
They will come out in their curious way
And be my friends every day.
They go up on their hind legs and look so cute,
They'd be good at playing the flute.

Hannah Cousins (11)
Heathfield School

WHY?

Between two worlds my heart must choose
But either way my heart must lose,
The world of glitz, beauty and glam
Or the world of me.

Always morphing to fit the puzzle,
Swimming in a sea of debacle,
Conscience clanging at the bars of sanity,
My heart is weeping,
Why?

Dastardly deeds are forced upon those
Who discard and who oppose,
Worries manifest into visions of demons
Plotting your undoing
By thy side.

Hold my head up high,
Face pain until the night,
One relief is obtainable,
Sweet release from life,
My heart does cry!

Jessica Kangalee (13)
Heathfield School

MY FANTASY WORLD

I have a wonderful fantasy world in my mind,
My head is full of magical creations
It is going to explode with these thoughts
Like an amazing display of fireworks,
A world of unicorns, fairies and goblins,
Dwarves, elves and sorcery
Where magic spreads everywhere,
Through the forests, mountains, skies and seas.

I have a bright vision of this world,
As clear as crystal, as clear as glass,
The mountains are spacious and colossal
Overlooking this wondrous place
Whereas the forests are dangerous and un-welcome
With goblins and evilness at every corner.
This magical cosmos is gorgeous and wonderful
But has its wicked times full of darkness.

In the seas lie mermaids with glossy fish tails
And attractive fantastic fish,
The wind and waves race together
And when they meet and crash, it sends a mighty outburst of water,
Winged horses fly through the open air
And phoenixes with golden tails,
If lucky you may see a dragon, once out of its cave
This beauteous creature may shine from a distance like a shooting star.

All the wonderful creatures soaring all around,
All the magical areas; green, blue and brown.
The magic, the fantasy is waiting for someone,
For someone to enter and take adventure in this spellbinding world,
People may think I'm insane
But I know that deep down this creation exists,
My creation is real in my head,
It will stay like that, forever.

Yasmin Afnan (11)
Heathfield School

THE LUCKIEST THING TO HAVE?

Mum
The luckiest thing to have on Earth is a mum and dad.
Mum is the one who bears the sweetest name in the family.
It is whom I as a child can say all she has is her heart.
Her love is a never-ending fountain.
It is she who feels the pain when the child is sick.
Indeed there is no one like her in the world.

Dad
Dad is like an army general whose heart is full of love.
He has a tough appearance.
He is the most reliable person and is a great leader.
All official work is his duty and never is it realised how much
He is looking after the child's welfare, schooling and hundreds of
                                        other problems!
He is also the cuddly bear
And is full of laughter!
He is just great!

Deepali Sangani (11)
Heathfield School

People In Many Different Ways

There are so many different types of people,
Sad, happy, angry, silent and loud.

You see some people so dull in the corner,
Never happy, never joyful.

You see some people who are always in the middle,
Having fun and enjoying their life.

You see some people always angry
Who want their way and never listen to other people.

You see some people always quiet,
Never talk or let out their emotions.

You see some people who are loud,
Who speak what they feel and shout.

All of these people are very different
And all these people have different personalities,
But all of them are slightly alike,
They are all humans and have every right to live.

Krupa Thakrar (12)
Heathfield School

Silence

In silence you can hear things, hark:
The whispering ladybird as it hurries,
The tapping woodpecker pecking on tree bark;
The rustling field mouse as it scurries
Through papery grass to nest beyond
And the plopping raindrop into the pond.

Pavetha Seeva (11)
Heathfield School

CONSERVATION

Brrrrr . . . came the deafening sound of a monster coming to eat it up.
Sudden, silent, waiting for the monster to arrive.
Turning to hear the monster heading towards me.
With the help of humans, it eats all of it down.
Looking around, animals fleeing from their habitats.
The animals are in danger, the small insects to the larger chimpanzee
All fleeing together.

Causing devastation to the peaceful world.
The outstanding cries, the dramatic bellows, all waiting ahead.
In a few minutes this part will be eaten by the deceiving monster.
Waiting, as it comes closer I suddenly move away.
When it had been eaten, the light came swimming in.
Why eat them harmless living things, destroying natural nature.
Will this ever come back again?

I turn around sadly to go home, spoiling my visit.
The next day I come, if there was any change.
Heart-broken by the view.
Why? The hard-hearted monster did this.
All buildings nasty man built buildings with a roaring fire in the middle.
Burning the rest of it.
They will be punished by God one day.

Covering all the nature, with dirty pieces of rock.
How many shopping centres does this planet need?
Maybe a thousand by the look of things.
How long this will take?
Why are they doing this?
I have many questions to ask.
This crazy monster destroys the unity of love on this planet.

Have a think, why are the monsters eating them? What is 'them'?
Think for yourself . . .

Briyandy Sivapathasundram (11)
Heathfield School

THE FLUFF BALL

Leo is my dog . . .
> He eats like it's the end of the world,
> He is warm when it is cold,
> He gives us exercise by his walks,
> He barks like mad to the dog next door.

But sometimes he . . .
> Chews up slippers,
> Eats the food on the table,
> Wets himself in the house,
> Tries to get the hamsters.

But when he's . . .
> Too sleepy to do anything,
> Only wants to eat,
> Tries to run away,
> Goes mad with his toys.

But I like him because . . .
> He's not too big,
> He's not too small
> And another thing is
> He's my little fluff ball!

I love my dog
> And you'd love him too
> But he's so special,
> I'm not sharing my
> Fluff ball with you!

Helena Manchester (11)
Heathfield School

WINTER

I like the winter because
We have to get out our wellington boots.
We have to wrap up in our warm clothes and we all look funny.
We have to take our umbrellas out of the cupboard.
We have to change our summer coat to our winter coat.
We also have to start taking vitamin C tablets so we don't catch colds.

I also like winter because
We get Christmas holidays.
We have a Christmas dinner
And we also get a nice Christmas meal for lunch at school.
We wear our Christmas hats and we do some crackers.
We also give and receive presents from other people.

Winter is special to me because
If it snows I love going to play in it,
It's really fun and I like throwing snowballs.
I also find it fun walking through a path covered in crispy leaves.
The sky changes colour, for example it changes from blue to pink.
The days get shorter so when I go to sleep it's really dark
And I can get to sleep quicker.

It is also special because
My grandpa's and my dad's birthdays are on the 1st and 2nd of January.
I get to spend time with my family
And we sometimes go on holiday.
I also get to meet up with my friends.
I just really like *winter!*

Deepa Kothari (12)
Heathfield School

HUMAN EXPERIMENTS

Lying awake in my world
Of solitary confinement,
Hundreds of us
Cramped in here,
Our heads poking through
A space just large enough
To fit in a rabbit's head.
'They don't matter.'
'Too many of them.'
'Blessed pests.'
Is there really a need for this?

A tall figure
Bending low
Examines a test tube filled
With yellow soap formula.
It straightens up slowly,
Approaches victim number one,
My brother.
Nose twitching obviously
And then he's gone.

Seconds later
The thing moves on,
Calls at number two
Does Doctor Death.
Surrounds him,
Inevitably this one flinches,
Needle inserted
And then he's gone.

Perspiration drowns me,
Nose twitching uncontrollably,
Moves on to me,
I flinch apprehensively,
Needle inserted -
And now I'm gone.

Week later product appears,
'Sollwells Finest Soap',
Totally pure.
This product has been thoroughly tested.
On who, I wonder?
An innocent rabbit, perhaps?

Lucy Shave (11)
Heathfield School

HEARTACHE

When he walked out of the front door
My heart it broke into a thousand pieces,
Like a crystal figurine crashing to the hard, cold marble ground
Which my soul has become.
My life has become a void of meaning, happiness, love.
Hope entirely has been removed from my life,
The light that used to shine at the end of my tunnel has left
And all my eyes can see is a deep, dark depression.
My head it pounds with thoughts,
Evil thoughts that mock me to sleep.
I feel sick with the pain.
The heartache grows with each day I don't sense you near me.
The scent of your cologne is fading in the bedroom
Which reminds me how long it's been since I held you in my arms.
The sound of your voice echoing in the corridors has been turned
Into a distant memory,
A sweet, faint memory and as I drift into my deep thoughts I realise that
When the smell of your cologne goes and your voice stops ringing in
My ears all I'll have to remember you by is the heartache that you
have left me with.

Natasha Misri (13)
Heathfield School

ASPIRATIONS

I'd promised myself and everyone else
To do my best at school.

I'd swot and slave and scrape and save
Until the place at the top was mine.

When I got to the top
I sat up straight, looked around and gloated.

I was sure I'd stand the test of time,
Sure I'd stay up floating.

A month or so ago I found myself floating to the bottom,
The work and the social life seemed to merge.

I couldn't wait till next year to start all over again,
So I picked myself up, I knew I had a plan.

So I slogged and sweated
And drudged and wore my brain dry.

I realised that it's alright to come in second place,
I grasped that in life only with yourself is it a race.

Leanna Christie (13)
Heathfield School

SILENCE

Silence is when you can hear things.
Listen:
The crunching of a ladybird as it munches crispy leaves;
The bashing of a robin as it walks along the branch;
The thudding of a squirrel as it jumps from one branch to another;
And the chiming of the moon as it comes out at night.

Safoora Kamal (11)
Heathfield School

ENCHANTED

In forests as ancient as the hills
Where no one dares go hunting,
In fear of creatures with pointed ears,
Having eerie faces and unknown powers.

In a stream
Some make their home
Among the mighty rock boulders,
Driving dragonflies for aeroplanes
Whilst surfing on autumn leaves in the water ripples,
But never sleep, do they nor night, nor day
Fearing intruders coming their way.

On the highest rock
In the stream
Sits their grand fairy queen,
Dressed in robes and acorn crown
She sits there elegantly all day round
Awaiting troubles to come her way
Until her people are all happy and gay.

Geetika Shah (13)
Heathfield School

SILENCE

Butterflies are flapping their wings
through the gentle breeze;
Robins tap their feet as they sway
along the branches;
Rabbits thump as they hop
on the ground
And then the moon slides in
as the sun sets.

Natalie Wijesundera (11)
Heathfield School

SHIVER, SHAKE!

As I walk through a dark alley,
Shiver, shake!
I hear footsteps gradually getting louder,
I see shadows approaching me.
What shall I do?

I walk faster thinking I was in danger,
Shiver, shake!
I feel like someone's breathing down my neck,
Or someone's getting closer.
Who could it be?

I hide myself in my black coat,
Shiver, shake!
I taste a dull sweetness in my mouth,
I smell a strong smell behind me.
Why is this happening to me?

As a gust of wind hits my face,
Shiver, shake!
I see a little child,
All alone,
Crying.
Was this my mind playing up?

As I run through a narrow bridge,
Shiver, shake!
I see a full moon above me,
Glowing,
Trying to tell me something.
Is this a bad sign?
Am I in danger?

Yasiga Kamal (12)
Heathfield School

MY FOE

My best friend
turned into my foe.
What could I do,
just forget it happened?

I cried and cried and cried
but nothing I could
say could change it,
my best friend
had turned away from me
and I had to face it.

Me broken into tears
but her not caring
what happened.
Just thought she
could throw it away
but with me it's not easy.

I wish and wish
one day we could
be best friends again
but I won't be able
to forget it.

One day she will suffer
and need someone,
someone like me
but then she will
realise there isn't
any more of me.

Toral Shah (13)
Heathfield School

HOLIDAYS

Barbados
Sun, the hot weather.
Beach, the silky sand beneath your toes.
Eating sugar cane, peeling off the hard stem
And enjoying the sweetness.
Sandcastles, building and toppling mounds of sand.

New York
Cold breeze, the icy breeze that covers New York.
Lots of people, the hustle and bustle of New York.
Busy streets, busy people on their way to do important things.
Massive shopping centres, the wonderful clothes at cheap prices.
Friendly people, always willing to give you a hand.

Denmark
Warm weather, the sunny weather.
Statues, the little mermaid by the harbour.
Theme park, riding the oldest wooden roller coaster in the world.
Hotels, the hospitality of the Danish people.
Food, the wonderful Danish dishes.

Orlando
Theme parks, roller coasters and water rides that take your breath away.
Roller coasters, great arched swings that defy gravity.
Junk food, stuffing yourself with junk food, corn dogs and
                                                    lots of sweets.
Hot dogs, sausages in a bun with mustard or ketchup splashed on.
Heat, the sunny weather making you sweat.

Washington DC
White House, the famous building where American presidents live.
Family, visiting relatives and going out on outings together.
Sight-seeing and taking photographs of famous buildings,
Postcards, buying cards and boasting to friends about your
terrific holiday.
Lots of sun, the orange ball of light warming you.

Alicia Matheson (11)
Heathfield School

WHEN?

We all live in this world,
A place where poverty and famine feed on feeble lives,
Where war plays its role from day to day,
When will peace arrive?

Hunger lies in the eyes of millions -
So weak, so vulnerable.
One drop of thick, misty water, searched for day after day.
When will death stop stealing lives?

Thousands face the pain like that of a million needles.
Still, the grief never fades.
Scarred by war, scarred by others,
When will the hurt be sent away?

The two giant brothers stood tall and proud,
Strike 1! Strike 2! Fire blazed like Hell in the skies.
Universal landmarks reduced to rubble,
Terror had feasted its eyes on the west.

Anguish and torment . . . will there ever be an end?

Seema Allahdini (13)
Heathfield School

DREAMS

Some dreams are precious pictures to remember and keep,
These are the dreams that bring back the best memories,
Or show you everything you've ever wanted to see.
But when you wake up, the amazing things you've just seen
                                        are forgotten in a flash,
Gone forever, dissolved into nothingness.

There are also other types of dreams,
These are ones that startle you awake in your bed.
The ones that show you the things you've never imagined,
The ones that show you the things you've never wanted to see,
The ones that warn you where and when the next tragedy will be.

Dreams are mysteries that can never be solved.
Some people spend a lifetime searching for their meaning,
Others think dreams are meaningless,
Pictures to scare and trick you.
What do *you* think? What do *you* dream?

Amy Fehilly (11)
Heathfield School

SILENCE IS WHEN YOU CAN HEAR THINGS: LISTEN

Silence is when you can hear things: Listen:
The slithering sound of a snail sliding across the ground,
Leaving a shimmering mark behind it;
The sudden flutter of a sparrow's wings
As it dodges his predator;
The violent rustling as a squirrel scurries up a tree
And a whisper of a tree as it sways delicately in the wind.

Danielle Falk (11)
Heathfield School

DREAMS

How come when you want to dream,
Lying on your bed,
Wishing you couldn't hear
The whoosh of the tank,
Or the creak of a floorboard,
You can't dream.
Instead you have nightmares
Of ghosts, monsters and bandits in disguise.

And how come when you don't want to dream,
Oh, that's a different story,
Sitting in a maths lesson,
Under the nose of a teacher,
Then you start to daydream
About sitting in your garden and eating an ice cream,
Or having a chat with a friend.
Then in the distance, you hear someone calling you,
Turning the words around in their mouth,
Something about maths.
Oh no!

Zainab Hakim (11)
Heathfield School

SILENCE

Silence is when you can hear things,
Listen,
The pounding of an ant's feet scurrying across the floor,
The stretching of a robin's wings ready to take flight,
The screech of a squirrel's claws scraping the tree as he climbs,
The crash of a grain of sand hitting the seabed.

Colette Fisher (12)
Heathfield School

MY MOTHER

My mother is a person who cares for me
And tucks me in at night.
When I make errors
She'd say it's alright.
She is the one who cares
And she will always shed most tears.
My mother is someone who comforts me
When I am in distress.
My mother cries when
I do something bad
And cries even harder when
I do something good.

My mother is like a volcano
About muddy puddles on the floor.
Like a prehistoric monster,
Like a car screeching
On a bad day.
My mother has to be in a hurry.
When the doorbell rings
The baby cries,
They all start at once.
My mother gets in a rage
Rushing all over the place.

Thank you, Mother,
It is not easy to express
What I would like to tell her.
For what goes on unnoticed
Every single day,
But still she is there
With all her understanding heart
And those never-to-be-forgotten
Words of advice.
She laughs when I laugh,
She cries when I cry,
She lives when I live.
I cannot say more about her
Except that she lives for me
And I live for her.

Mythiraye Ravinthiran (13)
Heathfield School

SILENCE!

Silence is when you can hear things.
Listen:
The crashing of a worm, racing through
The thick crispy soil;
The crunching of a robin, munching a
Worm anxiously;
The sniffing of a rabbit; watching out
For the fierce fox
And the crackle of a raindrop,
Spreading around the long rusty grass.

Nikita Shah (11)
Heathfield School

MY HOBBY

My favourite way
To spend the day
Is to go horse riding
On one of my friends, Sam or Monty
At my local RDA.

I have ridden in competitions,
National championships and regional shows.
I started when I was 3
And have won 3 cups, a shield and 25 rosettes,
Winning is important to me.

I have a mentor, Nikki
Who has same disability as me.
She rides with one hand only
And has an Olympic Gold Medal,
Well actually she's won 3!

I am training to achieve the highest standards
And to be a 2008 Paralympian,
Doing dressage, show jumping and eventing.
The challenges are very demanding
But also very rewarding.

My teacher, Clive
Is one of 15 trainers in the country
Who teaches disabled children to ride.
He's also the National Team Coach
And is always at my side.

Natasha Wait (11)
Heathfield School

A SNOWDROP'S LIFE

A rounded seed in the moist ground
All silent and peaceful till it awakes,
The stem bursts out through the ground,
A life is about to begin.

The stem unravels higher and higher,
It finally reaches the top
And out forms a bud all sealed and perfect,
Ready to open as a beautiful snowdrop.

In the morning sun with the dew sparkling bright
Hangs the new snowdrop,
So smooth, so delicate,
It's like a priceless crystal, just drooping in the fresh glowing light.

Its life's shortening,
It's withering and shrivelling,
Lowering to its heartbreaking death,
The magnificence is departing
Whilst darkness is just arriving.

Finally the end arrives,
The snowdrop falls to a stop
On the dry and parched ground,
Lying in a crunchy dismal state
And in an instant the life vanishes,
A life has just ended.

Sarah Mahgoub (12)
Heathfield School

MY ROOM

Cold, dark and isolated
That's how I feel when I walk in my room.
I long for freedom,
I feel enclosed and trapped,
I am a lonely prisoner.

I can't sleep at night,
I hear the clock ticking,
Tick-tock it goes.
1 minute gone,
Tick-tock I hear,
2 minutes gone,
I'm losing my mind.

I feel the walls enclosing on me,
I hug myself waiting for morning,
I see shadows,
I hear voices,
I'm scared and frightened.

I run out when morning comes,
I'm cold, stiff and sweaty,
I don't tell anyone,
I confine the information within,
I shower knowing I have to change,
I grab my clothes and run out,
I change outside my door.

I go downstairs to have my breakfast,
My family sees me shaking,
They ask questions, I don't answer,
I know they would only laugh
But I know what lies within my room.

I hate my room,
No one ever comes to my house.
I can't do anything because of it,
I have visions of evil things.

I come back from school and know what I have to do,
I go to my room and surrender,
It traps me,
I'm suffocating,
I'm losing my mind,
I lose my life,
I'm only 10.

Melanie Agyare (13)
Heathfield School

IF I COULD FLY

If I could fly,

I would taste the flames of the sun
    And bask in the light of the moon.

Grab the raindrops
    Before they bounce and make a sound.

Touch the fingertips of lightning
    And dance to the rumble of thunder.

Watch the people
    Holding onto the earth.

Listen to the clouds of sheep
    Bleat while they graze on the blue.

If I could fly
    I would dream
Of running on rivers
    And swimming on sands.

Lauren Schofield (13)
Heathfield School

WHICH DO I CHOOSE?

Many people like different colours,
Red, yellow, purple, green, white, black and blue,
But which do I choose?

Red is a powerful colour which tells you when to stop.
Sometimes red could be a passion of love like a precious rose.

Yellow is the sun shining on top of me, bright and heavily,
Glowing in my eyes.
It is a natural sense of colour that it sometimes makes me cry.

Purple is like the fast thinker. People say purple gives you strength,
Or helps you with your education.

Green is the envy that sometimes escapes from us,
Or green is the grass growing in the sun.

White is the angel flying in the sky with its wings open wide.
White is the cloud which moves away to let the sun come to us.

Black is like a stormy rain heading my way,
Sometimes black is a sad mood which gets into a bad day.

Blue is the clear sunny sky making the day look beautiful.
Blue is the sea swishing its waves from side to side as the wind
Gently blows in the fresh air.

But which do I choose?

Yalinie Sivapalan (11)
Heathfield School

TIME

I wait for guests to arrive,
I wonder if my watch has stopped,
Time drags on.

I'm laughing with friends,
We're chatting away,
Time flies by.

I daydream through class,
The teacher drones on,
Only half the lesson is gone.

I frantically scribble down answers,
I wonder if I'll finish the test,
Already half my time is gone.

I have places to go and people to see,
The holidays give me space to breathe,
Then suddenly they're over.

I loathe bad days,
Everything goes wrong right from the start,
They never seem to be over.

Time never does what I want,
Time only does what it will,
I suppose I should learn to accept
That time will never stand still.

Jessica Kim (13)
Heathfield School

MY IMAGINARY GARDEN

The sweet scent of the overpowering flowers,
Colours of vibrant crimson and daffodil gold,
The waving hands and smiling faces,
The swaying and dancing of plant life,
All waiting to be showered by my praise.

A faraway tune is constantly heard,
My deep blue river swerves and winds
Like an endless barren road,
I stare into its depths searching for an answer,
Only a mirrored face can be seen.

As I look up vines reach out to the sun,
Clouds form into animals,
Birds dive in silky skies,
Trees sprout out leaving patches of shade,
Apples fall into my hands.

The glossy shell of ladybirds
As they scuttle along the floor,
Glossy skins of various butterflies
Stream out like painted ribbons.

This is my sweet world,
My own imaginary garden.

Shan Luo (13)
Heathfield School

WHAT MY FAMILY THINKS ABOUT ME

My mum and dad think I'm precious,
My sister thinks I'm a pest.

My aunt and uncle think I'm wicked,
My cousin thinks I'm the best.

I think I'm funky,
I think I'm cool.

I love my family
And I think they rule.

Priyal Patel (12)
Heathfield School

MY LIVING WORLD

All creatures great and small,
Will end up dying if we pollute this Earth,
Car fumes, noise, litter,
What has this world turned to?

Sometimes I wonder and ask myself questions,
When will living things come to an end?
How will living things end?
What has this world come to?

Scientists, geographers,
Trying to find ways to safe life,
Animals, humans, insects and birds,
What has this world come to?

Families, friends.
Could this be our last day seeing them?
How would that feel?
What has this world come to?

All creatures great and small,
Will end up dying if we pollute this Earth,
Car fumes, noise, litter,
What has this world turned to?

Caitlin Davies (12)
Heathfield School

THE WAY I FEEL

My heart is my most fragile and precious thing,
Broken so easily by friends and foes alike.
It's my weakest point, my Achilles' heel,
The reason why I get so low.

I hurt so much yet I soldier on for others,
I like to be someone's shoulder to cry on,
Someone's rock, someone's ray of hope
To reason with them and make sure they'll be OK.

My life at the moment isn't great,
But when is it ever? Does anyone feel perfectly happy?
I sure don't feel down and mopey most of the time,
Wishing for things I can't have or are out of reach.

I want to wake every day with a spring in my step,
A reason to get up with enthusiasm not dread,
To love each moment I'm alive and fulfil my dreams,
For life to be a long happy ride, fantasy I know.

There's one person in my life
Who fails to acknowledge my feelings
Or feel how I feel but he's just so special,
Caring, sweet and loving, if only, but I can't live on that.

I want to love and be loved, especially by him,
My being, the centre of someone's universe.
Me for who I am brighten up someone's day
And my smile to make their week. The power of love!

Amy Morris (13)
Heathfield School

THE LAKE OF DREAMS

I'm dreaming by the lake again,
Of what I want to be,
I'm dreaming by the lake again,
The lake, where I feel free.

It's never ever just the same
At other lakes and streams,
It has to be the special one,
The special Lake of Dreams.

I'd like to be the grassy bank
That holds the crystal lake,
But not the muddy, dirty kind,
A bank is a mistake.

When the day is over
And I'm tired of shouts and screams.
The lake will help me to relax,
The special Lake of Dreams.

I'd love to be the crystal lake
Or the deep blue sea,
But I hate to get all wet,
Perhaps that's not for me.

I thought I could daydream all day
But maybe not, you see
I've realised after all the dreams
I'm happy being me.

Charlotte Campbell (12)
Heathfield School

THE WORLD

Have you ever stopped to think
What we have done to this world?

There is so much pollution
There have been so many murder cases
And rapes
And missing people

Have you ever stopped to think
What we have done to this world?

If there was no murder
No rapes
No missing people

People could open their doors
And not be scared that someone would hurt them

Have you ever stopped to think
What we have done to this world?

Estella King (12)
Heathfield School

LISTEN

Silence is when you hear things.
Listen!

The gentle vacuum of air when a spider breathes
Because it has been working hard to build its web;
The swoosh of air when the robin flaps its wings;
The cat makes a patting noise when it tiptoes
As it makes its way to its prey;
The explosion when a bud transforms into a beautiful flower.

Aysha Dhanani (11)
Heathfield School

HENRY

Henry was a happy man
Who lived with child and wife.
Many great men still don't know
What made him take his life.

For Henry the story starts
On an average day,
When off to work went Henry
And for this he would pay.

Whilst poor Henry worked
He never knew,
That at his home his wife and brother
Were together too.

On this afternoon he finished early
And went home to his lover,
Only to find her in their bed
With his only brother.

That night many tears were shed
As the ones he loved tried to explain,
But Henry's heart was already dead
He would never love again.

So Henry took his trusty gun
And held it to his head.
To relieve himself from this great pain
He pulled the trigger and soon was dead.

His wife she wept so deeply,
Her heart was heavy and sad.
Her careless actions had left her son
Without his loving dad.

Jessica King (13)
Heathfield School

DREAMS

I dream I'm on an island
Where the sun never dies,
Where the ocean glistens,
I see from above flying through the skies.

Each day I dream I'm somewhere special,
Sharing my thoughts with you,
Watching the sunset in peace,
Those little things matter too.

I dream I'm gliding through the sky,
Swooping as I fly.
I wish this dream would never end,
Never does time pass by.

I stay in my dream as long as I like,
This dream is only for me,
Never do I want to wake up,
Wake up in reality.

Georgina Parr (13)
Heathfield School

MY GRANDMOTHER

My grandmother is excellent
She helps me a lot
She sometimes shouts at me
But she is the nicest person I have got

She is not very quiet
And can't keep her mouth shut
She talks about nice things
But it is annoying and that is the only *but!*

She is very chubby
And is sixty-seven
But she runs around like a teenager
And looks like she is eleven

I love my grandmother
And she loves me too
But now I have to end this poem
Because my grandmother is about to serve me some food!

Nirooba Sivanesan (12)
Heathfield School

Fantasy Land

In a land far away, there are children who dream
They could play there all day.
They dream night after night,
Looking for the wonderful light.

This fantasy land is fun,
Where you can talk and run.
When you are there, you can waste your time,
Playing in fields the colour of lime.

This land is huge and beautiful,
It is also very colourful.
It is lovely and bright
And there are never any fights.

In the land far away, which you dream about all day,
It is called Fantasy Land.

Shreya Patel (11)
Heathfield School

MY BROTHER

S accharin sweet he looked, a dream come true,
H e had been born, as I had craved and had wished too.
A baby brother was something I always desired,
   and now I had acquired him blithely.
B rother or doll? I asked myself as I touched his smooth skin gently,
B lue were his eyes, dark like the ocean, when he cried
I saw my own reflection reflecting in his dark blue eyes,
   gazing back at me mystified,
R ejoicing in this day, the happiest day of my life.

M onths have gone by of snuggling and cuddling the cute little child,
Y ears have flown and now he is not so mild.

B ig blue eyes have been converted by the turquoise of the ocean,
   glistening back to you,
R aucous and ebullient he has become and has a mind of his own too!
O ver, where his minuscule little lips used to be now he wears a
   mischievous grin,
T all and adventurous he has become and every challenge he will win!
H e is now nine, going on ten, he's the boss of the house! So never
   mess with him!
E ither he's laughing one minute and angry the next, so stay away
   when he has a mood swing!
R avishing and funny my brother is, we have our brawls and fights but
   overall I love him!

Zahra Jamaluddin (14)
Heathfield School

MY CAT

Her bold deep eyes glare without blinking,
Staring and watching, carefully thinking.
She licks her lips and stretches out her claws,
Keeping quiet she moves forward on one paw.

She swipes her tail ready to pounce,
She wants her meat, she wants her mouse.
With one leap and a cry so shrill
Her claws dig in, she's got her kill!

Amina Sadiq (13)
Heathfield School

THE CRAFTY CROC

The crocodile sits in the slimy swamp,
Ready,
Eager
To pounce on its prey.
The long, cruel tail shakes as it sweeps.
Slowly,
Alert,
It lunges!
Prey being dragged,
Helplessly,
Defenceless,
From the river bank,
Unable to escape
The powerful jaws of its predator,
Whose teeth cut through flesh,
Crush bone with ferocity.
The crocodile,
Shrewd, wild beast,
Its dry, scaly skin against rocks,
Camouflaged,
Only moving for its own benefit,
To bask in the sunlight.

Paula Strauss (13)
Heathfield School

DREAMS

Nothing should ever take your heart away from what you want to do,
Dreams are real for everyone, you need to do what's best for you.
If you keep believing that a dream will come true,
No matter how unreal it may seem there is a chance in there for you.
Everyone has a time in life where all their dreams come true and one
Day everything you have ever wished for will be right in front of you.
When this time comes all you have to do
Is take what comes, be happy with it and do what's best for you.
A dream is a thought that stays on your mind, something that
                                                  you long for.
A dream is something that you keep wanting more and more and more.
One day in many years to come your dreams will follow through
And on that one day you will find that dreams can become true.

Jenny Graham (13)
Heathfield School

FRIENDS

A friend is there to make you smile,
To make you laugh
And to make you cry.

Friends stay with you through thick and thin,
They are your shoulder to cry on when you are down,
They are always there to have a joke with and to tease.

We turn to friends for advice,
For a chat
And for a good time.

Everyone needs a friend
And I am so lucky that I have found you
Because you are one of a kind.

Vicky Estruch (12)
Heathfield School

MY ROOM

My room is the best place I could be,
Filled with toys and things for me.
I have a desk where I do my work
And a radio so I can listen to music.
I have lots of posters and photos all around
Which remind me of the people I love.
Along the wall is my bed, which is big and comfy,
With a cosy duvet to snuggle under.
My wardrobe sits in the corner covered in half torn stickers,
A legacy from my sister when she shared my room.
My toy box full of memories from years ago
And ornaments all over my shelves.
To keep me in touch with my friends there is a phone
With my own number so I'm never alone.
But my room is my own private space,
It is mine where I can do what I want,
My world.
All that's missing is a television,
An en-suite bathroom
And a fridge!

Lucy Riseborough (13)
Heathfield School

LISTEN

Silence is when you hear things.
Listen:
The gentle clicking sound when a ladybird eats its leaf;
The sweet and peaceful singing of the robin on a tree branch;
The soft tapping of a slow tortoise walking;
The swaying of a leaf that has been blown by the wind.

Prina Patel (11)
Heathfield School

My Loss

There he lies in that coffin.
The only thing that made teenagehood fun,
As you look back on the times you shared
You shed a tear,
For all things you wish you hadn't said
And all the things you wish you had,
You laugh
At all the fun you shared
And all the funny things you had done,
But the thing that upsets you most is
Knowing he isn't alive any more.

Everyone is telling you he isn't really gone
And you're never on your own,
Because he will come back in spirit
And look after you,
You know that's true
But you don't want him in spirit,
You want him in person
Because his spirit can't take you to places,
You want him to tell you
You're his little angel
And that you always will be.

The first night without him
You feel empty and lonely,
You start to cry because he isn't there
And you wish he was there to comfort you,
You try and stop
Because you know he wouldn't want to see you like this,
If you could have him back today,
If you could lose this pain and sorrow
You would just do anything,
You remember you'll always be his little angel
And it makes you feel a bit better,
But it's not the same.

You start to cry silently,
You start to cry a river inside
Because you wish you had told him how much
You love him and how much he means to you,
And that no one can replace him,
And you will never forget him,
And you won't even try,
You hope he knows how much you miss him.

Gemma Peat (13)
Heathfield School

WALKING HOME IN THE DARK

In the daytime I feel safe and warm,
Walking in the sunlight I always feel at home.

But walking in the dark
That's what gets my heart racing,
All these unfamiliar things I am facing.

Whether they are big and whether they are small
It really doesn't seem to matter at all.

My mind plays tricks on me,
Making everything seem worse,
Sometimes I think this fear is a curse.

This fear gnaws inside you and never leaves you alone,
The only place I can face my fears is at home.

Rachael Capper (12)
Heathfield School

IF I HAD WINGS . . .

If I had wings
I would fly high into the sky
And dance on the cloud tops.

If I had wings,
I would race to the above
And meet the God that watches us below.

If I had wings,
I would snatch a speck of the sun
And use it to guide me through the night.

If I had wings,
I would rise over the oceans
And watch the creatures that whirl within.

If I had wings,
I would gasp at the sight
Of the wickedness that I left behind . . .

If I had wings,
I would fly away.

Melania Ishak (14)
Heathfield School

MY FANTASY LAND

A far-off land like no other,
It is a land you would never discover.
It is a serene and joyous place,
This is my fantasy land.

This is a strange and spectacular land
With extraordinary creatures
And unusual colours,
That is my fantasy land.

It is a place where you can relax
And you can be released from your fears,
Where all your troubles just disappear,
That is my fantasy land.

This marvellous and beautiful land of mine
One day I hope to find,
It is a place where anything is possible,
This is my fantasy land.

Kaveeta Sonigra (12)
Heathfield School

FEARS

I have a fear of pockets,
I'm scared when I reach in.
It is so deep and dark,
The secret is within.

I hate to think what's inside,
I really cannot tell.
It might be ferocious spiders
Or even monsters from Hell.

I love the way my trousers are made
But the pockets spoil it all.
I look for ones without pockets
But none is at the mall.

I have a fear of pockets,
It brings me lots of tears.
This is one of my stories
About one of my fears.

Tara Wignadasan (12)
Heathfield School

SUMMER

The sun's always glistening on your skin,
Birds singing sweetly,
Daisies blooming slowly,
Green leaves growing,
Summer holidays approaching soon,
Days getting longer,
Nights getting shorter,
Excitement building gradually,
Children play in gardens,
Bells of ice cream vans ringing merrily,
Hats and gloves being put away,
Shorts and T-shirts being taken out,
Even the darkest days are brighter with
The feeling of summer!

Sheenal Vasani (13)
Heathfield School

SILENCE

Silence is when you can hear things.
Listen:
The slurping of a worm slowly
Slithering through the damp soil;
The flapping of a bird's wing
Eager to get to its destination;
The hamster crawling through
The sawdust in its cage;
The drip of a drop of water
Falling down to the ground.
Silence!

Shreena Vakani (11)
Heathfield School

AUTUMN

Autumn is here
When the crispy leaves fall off the trees,
The colours of autumn are
Oranges, yellows, reds and pinks.

As the leaves swirl around in the wind
They dance around trees and branches,
Swinging to and fro
With the crispy sounds they make.

Most people don't notice its beauty
But I certainly do,
It slowly gets colder
As it approaches the winter.

Katherine Ford (12)
Heathfield School

ANGELS

I believe in angels,
I believe I am yours,
I believe I'm your angel
Sent here to open closed doors.
I believe I can help you
Every step of the way,
I'm always there
Throughout the day.
I believe I'm your angel,
Together we become
A force that lasts
As long as the sun.

Emily Carr (13)
Heathfield School

LIFE

People believe in different things
From when they are born until the end,
But life at this moment could be improved
But many people do not comprehend.

Life is a very fragile thing,
Tender like petals on a flower
But if you destroy this delicate life
You could lose it within the hour.

To live is extremely exciting,
It is an adventure for you to explore,
But sometimes people do not realise what they have,
So they keep on wanting more.

Sometimes you think that life is too short,
Too short for doing pointless things,
Others like to take some risks,
So they feel like they're flying without wings.

Some people are bullied for what they wear,
Others because of their skin,
However, I would like to know why they are
As we are all the same within!

Jennifer Parr (13)
Heathfield School

ROSES ARE RED

Roses are red,
Roses are white,
Roses are pink and calm as the night.

Roses are kind,
Roses are gentle,
Roses aren't worth a lot, but sentimental.

Roses remind me of a summer's day,
Roses make me think of May,
Roses are happy,
Roses are cheerful,
Roses are bright and won't make you fearful.

Sophia Savitsky (13)
Heathfield School

SECRETS

Secrets, secrets
What shall I say
When I kept this from him
When he was far, far away.

Secrets, secrets
He was long, long gone
I wish I could tell him
By singing a song.

Secrets, secrets
It is very important
Through the maze
Find your way
And come and play.

Secrets, secrets
It lies beneath
It's the end of the way
I wish he was here
But he left me and ran away.

Farah Khan (12)
Heathfield School

MUSINGS OF A MIRROR

This is me
This is who I am
A mirror
I am cold and cruel
I hate who I am and I hate what I do
She is my friend yet I am her enemy.

She slowly looks at me
And I show her reflection
Gentle tears leave her eyes
As she turns around and walks away.

What have I done I ask myself
Except be honest to my dear friend?
I try to reach out to her
I feel her pain
But who am I?
Just another mirror.

Deepa Lakhani (12)
Heathfield School

SILENCE

Silence is when you can hear things.
Listen:
The slush of a snail as it slowly slithers along;
The splashing of the blue tit's tongue as it hits the water;
The rustle of the field mouse as it sleeps in its cosy nest
And the tear of a petal as it falls from a flower.

Alisha Patel (11)
Heathfield School

SEASONS

Spring is here at last,
Pink flowers start to unfold,
Rabbits appear out of their holes, from their long sleep.
In quiet waters, fishes start to sing,
Whilst nature starts to grow.

Summer is when the sun opens up,
Umbrellas of the trees, of the leaves, make a shade.
May the days go fine and
Red nights are here to end it all.

Autumn leaves start to fall,
Down they tremble to the ground.
Trees are left bare and cold,
Days get shorter, there's not a minute for you to lose.

Winter comes to unravel its cold,
Snow falls heavily.
Close the curtains to close out the darkness,
Light the fire to bring in the warmness.

Nishma Malde (11)
Heathfield School

SILENCE

Silence is when you can hear things, listen:
Listen to the ant thumping its way through the long, crunchy grass.
Listen to the bird screeching out to others for attention.
Listen to the rabbit pounding its way down the rocky path.
Listen to the sun burst into the sky and start crackling
to everyone's attention.

Mishri Amin (11)
Heathfield School

FEAR

Fear is in my nightmare
Which scares me when I wake
To think I've lost a loved one
To whom someone had to take

Or when I'm all alone
To no one I can speak
I find myself frightened
I think I've skipped a beat

Or when I'm in the darkness
There is no light in sight
I feel someone is watching me
And give myself a fright

The only time I feel safe
Is when I'm in loving care
Of my friends and family
Without them I'd go spare.

Melanie Dhanaratne (12)
Heathfield School

SILENCE

Silence is when you can hear things, listen:
The buzzing of a small fly as it flies through the moonlit sky;
The beat of a blue tit's wings flapping through the hot summer;
The padding of a hamster's feet hitting the sawdust in its cage
And the twinkling of the stars as they shine in the night.

Mehreen H Kassam (11)
Heathfield School

MY GARDEN

The sun beams down on the freshly cut grass,
Droplets on leaves shine like polished glass,
The sun-yellow dandelions proudly face the sky
And the young rainbow coloured butterflies flutter and fly.
Every flame-shaped leaf shivers on, so quietly
And the neighbour's cat creeps about the garden slowly.
The speckled sparrows sweetly sing their whistling tunes
And slowly but surely the caterpillar slides out of his cocoon.
The wonderful aroma of the flowers, blue, pink and red,
Was as if perfume had been sprinkled, along each flower bed.
The dainty aphids danced across the delicate roses
But here a spotted ladybird arrives, a threat she poses.
I see a black and yellow, busy, buzzing creature, it is a bumblebee,
Then I sorrowfully realise it is time to go in now for tea.

Douriya Jodiyawalla (13)
Heathfield School

LISTEN!

Silence is when you hear things.
Listen:

Listen to the scuffling of an army of ants struggling across the ground.
Listen to a robin swooping down like a plane
and grabbing a slithering worm in her beak.
Listen to a squirrel struggling into her warm and cosy nest.
Listen to the *pop* of a bud blooming into a dazzling flower.

Leila Chawla (11)
Heathfield School

DREAMS

Before I go to bed I close my eyes and dream,
A pitch-black starry night
With the cool breeze blowing on your face
Or maybe I am on a boat drifting away
On the clear blue sea,
Or even in the damp green jungle
Fighting for my life,
Maybe I am in the boiling desert
Sweating like crazy,
Sometimes I dream that I am
A millionaire and I can do whatever I want,
I can dream of anything and everything,
Smart owls, purple ducks,
Flying dogs, swimming cats
As long as it's a dream.

Dami Sunmonu (12)
Heathfield School

ICE CREAM MANIA

As you bring the ice cream closer to your mouth,
all your taste buds begin to shout,
'Come in, come in and infuse us with your flavour,'
Whether it's a vicious vanilla,
Sweet strawberry,
Bizarre banana,
Guzzling grape, or even a pleasant pear,
The ice cream doesn't really care.
As the ice cream melts in your mouth,
All the flavours come rushing out.

Leena Patel (11)
Heathfield School

THE NEXT STEP

As I stand at the gate looking nervous and scared,
Six long weeks of relaxation have come to an end,
Butterflies do loop-the-loop in my stomach,
I am all alone and wonder if I will find a friend.

Heading to the classroom, dragging all our bags,
Twenty of us alike in our uniform, crisp and new,
Trying to remember names and our way around the place,
Waiting for instructions to tell us what to do.

Teachers introduce themselves, trying to grasp our names,
Timetables, class rules and textbooks to collect.
Over-brimming desks, when is break? And what's for lunch?
A few moments to spend with the friends I have met.

Isabelle Tranter (11)
Heathfield School

NEVER JUDGE A BOOK

Oh, you may not think I'm pretty,
But don't judge on what you see.
I'll renew myself if you can find
A smarter book than me.
So just pick me off the shelf
And read my first few chapters,
For then you'll really see
How smart a book I can really be!
There's nothing hidden in my pages
You're not allowed to read,
So open me up and I will tell you
Where you start to read . . .

Zara Chung (11)
Heathfield School

THE SECRET

At first only two of us knew
but by Tuesday it was being
passed around like a game of
Chinese whispers.

The next day everyone knew
about it and there was nothing
we could do, we had betrayed her
trust and now the secret was out.

We all knew it would end in tears
and broken hearts to the girl we
had deceived that very day.

Even though we regretted we didn't
stay silent the belief of it all was too much
and now the truth was finally out.

Roxanna Baker (14)
Heathfield School

THE SEA

The tranquil blue serenity is light.
The sky an everlasting peaceful blue.
Diamonds within it sparkle day and night,
Full of precious glistening jewels cruising too.

A space of blue so vast will never end.
'Tis like a heaven but 'tis down here.
A lively gift from God to us descend,
Does this wondrous gift ever die?

A smear of white and blue so violent yet so calm,
So evil like a devil but 'tis blue.
Consists of waves so bad it draws a fight,
So bad without a heart it kills you through!

I love this peaceful everlasting glee,
I hate this blue cold devil called the sea.

Sharmili Balarajah (15)
Heathfield School

LOVE

Love can do many strange and painful things,
The hurt, the pain, the doubt and numerous tears.
Is love really pointless, or just for rings?
It carries many doubts, feelings and fears.

Yet it can bring gleaming smiles and bliss,
Happiness, presents and lovely times.
All for that passionate, amazing kiss,
Which leads to white dresses, cakes and chimes.

The single life is also to enjoy,
To dance, to flirt with whom you choose,
To look stunning and glamorous for a boy,
There's always some to gain, and some to lose.

Love means a thousand incredible words,
It's wonderful to be just two lovebirds.

Janki Rabheru (15)
Heathfield School

AWAITING

I remember:

Clean cut rounded fingernails,
The smell of flowers in spring,
A voice as sweet as an angel,
Strawberry redness in her lips,
Smiles curved as in a banana
And glossy chestnut hair.

Butterflies
Scurrying around her,
Raindrops coming to an end,
Sunshine surrounding her
And the stars always sparkling.

The caring qualities of a mother,
Calmness in her path,
Her mane was like a lioness,
Her footsteps of a ballerina.

Sometimes she was clumsy,
Sometimes she was silly,
But always and forever she was full of energy.

Over the hills and mountain tops,
Past the houses and seas,
Near the sparkling, shimmering stars,
Beyond the thick blue clouds

I wait for her return . . .

Carmen Liu (13)
Heathfield School

THE BIG BLUE SEA

I got closer and closer to the pool,
Thinking, should I do it and be a fool?
My friends shouting, 'Go on you can do it!'
But they don't know the feeling not even a bit.

My foot touched the gentle warm water,
I went inside and got wetter and wetter.
I held the float in front of me,
The swimming pool looked like the sea.

My instinct told me, 'You have to do it!'
While my mind was saying, 'Don't you'll blow it!'
I decided that I had to go,
I started kicking to and fro.

I kicked the water hard with my feet,
And went slowly from shallow to deep.
Surprisingly, I felt really great,
Especially with the support from my mates.

It was tiring as I kicked and kicked,
I was thinking, wow, I need to get fit!
I came closer and closer to the end,
Slowly closer to my friends.

I felt something hard and, *bump!*
I had reached the side with a thump!
I did it. Swam a length for the first time ever,
When I thought I would never do it, never.

Sarrumathy Sivanesan (14)
Heathfield School

THE HIGHWAYMAN

It was a dark and cold, windy night,
Not a star or twinkle of light in sight,
When over the marshes stood a man
In desperate need of a helping hand.

Upon his shoulders lay a dark black cloak
And he knocked upon the old inn door.
'I have travelled from afar,' he said,
'I need a place to rest my head.'
But not a sound came across the floor.

It was getting darker into the night,
Still the traveller stood outside,
He knew that someone was dwelling in the house,
He could sense their presence.
But as dawn drew near and the sun began to rise,
He gave up and left the old inn.
Little did he know that all along, inside was
The ghost of innkeeper Jim.

Clare Moore (13)
Heathfield School

NEVER-ENDING

When I see you my heart glows,
then I hear you and my heart grows.
When I think of you my heart leaps,
your friendship is what my heart keeps.

From our first hug to our last goodbye,
when I see you I'll still cry.
The time passes by, during the days
but when I'm with you the time always stays.

You're with me side by side,
to see me through thick and thin.
You mean the world to me,
and make our friendship flutter free.

We are like a circle, never-ending,
we stick together like glue.
You are like a petal, lenient, tender, and mind,
always there for me, when I am behind.

Shalina Patel (13)
Heathfield School

SUMMER TO WINTER

Summer's going and here comes winter,
Raging through the sun.

The weather gets cold, the trees are bare
And there is no more fun.

The animals scurry to and fro,
Not to be caught in the midnight air.

The trees are drooping, the birds cry out,
The water is frozen, the food is rare.

People don't go out as often,
So the atmosphere is softened.

Soon comes winter and the snow,
Houses warm with a cosy glow.

Sandani Chandrasekara (11)
Heathfield School

PEACE IS FAR, LOVE IS FURTHER

When I was young, my marriage seemed so far,
I never thought I'd ever be the bride
Walking down the aisle just like a star,
With so much love and joy stored up inside.

Love is something strong that cannot break,
A gentle thing that lives for evermore,
It's not like a glass that shatters with a shake,
there's nothing more in life that is so sure.

There's more to life than what we all expect,
Long days of work and very little rest.
There is no time to find someone perfect,
But then again, what is defined by best?

I write these lines with so much hope and glee,
Love I write, but love I cannot see.

Rushani Selvendran (14)
Heathfield School

HEATHFIELD SCHOOL

H   ow do you describe a school like this?
E   very child is friendly like this:
A   ll the six formers help you out,
T   eachers do when they are about.
H   ow do you describe a school like this?
F   irst, year seven the hard work begins,
I   t gets harder as the years go on,
E   nd of the day the hard work's done.
L   unch is okay if you have your own
D   inner awaits when you get home!

Aziza Phillips (11)
Heathfield School

MIRROR POEM

A lady looks into me,
Wondering who or what I am,
But I know who she is,
She doesn't know who I am.
She can't see me,
How will she react if she sees me?
She sees herself,
I want to talk to her.
If only she could see me,
She looks beautiful.
She's tying up her flowing hair,
She's in a hurry,
Why can't she just talk to me?
She can't see me,
But I trust her,
If only she could see me.

Lindsay Phillips (12)
Heathfield School

SILENCE

Silence is when you can hear things.
Listen:
The thunder of the dung beetle transporting his dung to his home;
The pounding of a blue tit skittering on the branch;
The thumping of a hamster's heart when he's running in his wheel
and;
The whining sound of a sycamore seed falling from the tree.

Jessica Agius (11)
Heathfield School

THE MOON

Between the willow trees,
The moon smiles down.
Happily guarding the Earth,
She never shows a frown.

Animals she helps,
To show them the way at night.
Smiling contentedly in the sky,
Her eyes shining bright.

When she is happy,
She beams downwards.
The moon is never angry,
She only beams outwards.

But when the morning comes,
She must hide away.
For her sister, the shining sun,
Is here to start a new day.

Bhavnisha Modi (11)
Heathfield School

ENVIRONMENT

The world was filled with beauty,
Such as never seen before.
Animals roamed of their own free will,
And lived in harmony.

But then one day through a forest went,
A young man on a donkey.
He said that he would build a town
With houses and a power station.

So this he did and in a year
His town was ready for people
He told his parents and all his friends
About his living arrangements

His parents and his friends
Were as delighted as he
But did they know the consequence
Of what the young man had done?

Bethany Wellington (13)
Heathfield School

OUR WORLD

What makes the world unhappy?
Why can't people just be friends?
What will happen in the future?
What if the world should end?

I don't understand the world,
Why does everyone want to fight?
Can't countries just be happy
Being side by side?

I wish I could make them see sense,
That happiness is best,
To get along together
Is a never-ending quest.

For future generations,
To live at last in peace
So that fighting wars and unhappiness
Will eventually cease.

Nicola Allen (13)
Heathfield School

THE SEASONS OF LIFE

Like springtime buds,
A fresh start
New beginning
Positive demeanour
New ambitions to set and goals to work on
so you can achieve what you want to achieve

Like summer flowers
At your best
Not a care in the world
Yet a will to do well
And a smile to brighten the sternest of faces
and to melt the iciest, coldest hearts.

Like autumn leaves
Falling from your height
Tension builds up around you
And the mistakes and the lies
Letting go of your power so slowly but surely
and landing with a thud as you hit the cold ground.

Like winter snow
Cold to the touch
A monotonous landscape
A life so mundane
But every day that passes, the promise grows stronger
like snowdrops pushing through the frost, spring will come again.

Sarah Turner (12)
Heathfield School

MY SECRET POWER

I have come round in the morning fully awake,
I feel first class, I know I will have been excellent.
I go to school and look at the exam,
Amazingly I was gobsmacked!
I obviously hit the jackpot,
100% wow! I had to tell my mum.
End of the day I was flat on the floor,
Knowing my mum will approach in half an hour.
Tick-tock, time was flying by,
It had been half an hour, it was half-past five!
In the car I was viewing dinner,
Knowing it will be pizza, superior, a winner!
Arrived at home and looked at the clock,
I established that it was seven o'clock!
Watched TV and did homework,
Mum was hectic in the kitchen since eight o'clock.
I am capable of sniffing that cheesy smell,
I can sense it fresh from the oven.
'Kids,' she would call,
I sprint for the pizza tumbling as I dash.
Pepperoni pizza, my desired pizza,
I slurp while I gobble it up.
Stuffing pizza in my mouth, watching TV,
I know I was departing for bed at ten forty-three.
Later after eating and watching TV,
And I go to bed at exactly ten forty-three.
Resting in my bed Mum says, 'Sweet dreams.'
Peace, harmony, tranquillity as I sleep,
Dream I was a doctor in a laboratory.
Now look at me I am Dr Sritharan,
And now I also know that I could predict the future!

Thivya Sritharan (12)
Heathfield School

FORGOTTEN

The sun, the sand, the sea,
People as happy as can be.
The warmth, the love and care,
The sense of belonging everywhere.

Do you know what place this is?
No, of course you don't, it is a country that has been missed,
This country is Iraq, a land forgotten,
Where people are sad and life is rotten.

Destroyed by strangers,
Invaded by enemies,
Deceived by friends
And stolen by thieves.

Demolished and ruined the once beautiful Iraq slowly wore away,
So that no one would speak of it forever, until today,
We held our heads high and stood with strength,
Rebuilding our homeland and achieving great lengths.

An amazing place once again restored,
We have all that we could have hoped for,
Hand in hand, heart to heart,
Nothing on Earth can tear us apart.

Iraq is my country, my love, my home,
Together united, never alone,
Iraq is my home, my love, my country,
Iraq is a land now filled with liberty!

Ayia Abbas (14)
Heathfield School

THE HORSES

A slither of silver moonlight
lay across the pitch-black field,
as the minutes turned to midnight,
'twas then the horses came.

Pure white were their bodies,
their manes whipped out behind them,
their eyes were full dilated,
their hooves made no sound.

These pearly, silent phantoms
galloped through the night.
A storm stirred above them,
as they took their flight.

The rain beat hard upon their backs,
the lightning cracked the sky.
They reared and kicked,
but kept on rushing by.

As they ran, the lands passed by,
from countryside to coast.
And when they met the ocean wide
their path it did not stop.

Their hooves left ground, they began to swim,
through the deep, blue water.
But then I blink, my eyes amazed,
for there they were no more.

Sarah Browne (14)
Heathfield School

SILENCE

Silence is when you can
hear things. Listen:
The sound of a beautiful
multicoloured butterfly
breathing and panting as
it rushes home in the cold breeze.
The sound of a small red and white robin's
heart thumping, as its little chest rises
and then goes down;
The creaking and crackling of the waves
as they twist round and round
crashing into each other with an enormous crunch;
The racing mind of a guinea pig,
trying to think, how to escape
from his four-legged friend.

Annika Dattani (11)
Heathfield School

WHAT ARE THEY?

They come in checks, they come in stripes
Their colours are bold and some are bright
They fly in the sky at day and night
With stars in the air or sun in the light
But when the air is strong like a tornado
The lightning strikes and the danger will flow
So when you go flying on them in the wind
The danger will strike when the lightning begins
So what are they?
They're air balloons of course, like birds in the wind.

Sammy Letham (11)
Orleans Park School

MY FAVOURITE BUILDING

My favourite building is a place where I can relax
A place where my emotions run wild
A place where I am allowed to do what I would like to do
A place where I can have some privacy

My favourite building is a place where my precious belongings are
A place where my secrets can hide
A place which will always be in my heart
A place where I can shut all of my worries out

My favourite place is a place where I will always be loved
                                          and welcomed
A place where I spend most of my time
A place which holds memories happy, sad and exciting
This precious place is my home.

Emma Deacon (11)
Orleans Park School

THE WIND

The willow trees whisper as the lake ripples.
The wind is dancing around, touching their surface with its hands.
The wind blows over the grass, making each stem stand on end.
The leaves dance with the wind as they fall off the trees.
As quiet as a mouse the wind moves in and out of their branches,
Blowing out the sun like a candle in the night,
Swishing and swirling all around.
Can you hear the musical sound
As it goes to rest in the ground?

Safiyya Hussein (12)
Orleans Park School

THE BUTTERFLY

The amazing colour
The delicate shape
It's there
You blink and it's gone
Back to the butter holes.

The flies get the colour from somewhere
'Where?' the children cry
'Down where we live!' answered the crumble bees
So down the young ones skipped
To the hives on berry hill
And when the farmer asked, 'Where are you goin' dears?'
They called back, 'To fetch a posy for dear Mama!'
And ran off happily.

The hives ahead of the crowd of babes
The children laughed with glee
We will at last have found the answer they all screamed
Tigers they were circling the hive
As they listened to the buzz inside.

They pounced and pulled on the lid of the hive
But then a thing happened
Too fast to see
And the children were gone
Still no one knows what happened
To the children.

Eleanor Massey (11)
Orleans Park School

MY FAMILY

My grandad was like a giant cuddly bear
His footsteps went thud, thud, thud.
When he threw me up it the air
It felt like I was flying until he caught me.

My brother is a little hot water bottle
He is always nice and warm
His weakness is food and computer games
He just never stops going.

My mum is beautiful and cool
She always says that she isn't
But I know that she is!
She is mad and stays up until 2am reading
Crazy person!

My nan is nuts, but she's cool (just like my mum)
She has just moved to Bournemouth
And now my auntie is living with us
My poor nan has had shingles and is
Still recovering
She is now a lot better though.

Even though there are only five
People in my family here
I think they're all really cool
Just like me!

Charlotte Cushen (11)
Orleans Park School

IN THE BREEZE

In the breeze my mind runs wild
With images wandering along the beach
Soon to cross the ocean soon to vanish
Soon I will not see them.

In the breeze my body goes cold
Standing towards the dark sea
It is all you see, like a big, fat ribbon
Bending towards you.

In the breeze my hair goes wild
Like it is dancing, dancing
Waving towards the sun
Turning against the sea.

In the breeze my fingers stiffen
Colder, colder
Until they are ice
So cold you cannot move them.

In the breeze I walk away
The breeze is a howling wolf
Until the sea has gone
Until the breeze has stopped.

Sophie Deacon (11)
Orleans Park School

BUNNIES HAIKU

Bunnies like to play
Twitching noses, fluffy bums
On a summer's day.

Sophie De Frond (11)
Orleans Park School

SMELLY FEET

There once was a man
I went to meet
Who had the smelliest ever feet.

We sat and stared
(and smelled of course!).
It put me off my chips and sauce.

I couldn't take it anymore
I ran straight to the main, front door.

I sprinted down the cobbled street
Into my house and put up my feet.

I shouted and screamed
and was horrified,
As my feet were becoming - fungified!

Alex McKenna (11)
Orleans Park School

WHITE HORSES

The waves were white horses,
The sky was pitch-black.
There was no star in the sky.
Neither boat nor ship dared to come near,
Not even to see the wondrous sight.

The deserted town was a tomb,
Silent as a grave,
No lights, no sound.
The rocks were giant statues.
But no one came,
No one,

Grace Rake (11)
Orleans Park School

ORLEANS PARK SCHOOL

Welcome to Richmond Road,
Welcome to the school.
Don't you dare wear the uniform
Because you will look like a fool.

Lessons are so cool,
And the teaches are as well.
The playground is so huge
But the hall is like a prison cell.

In English you will find,
The teachers are never far behind.
In maths you will see
The teacher whizzes around like a bumblebee.

In music you're to hear
Loud pop music, deafening the ear.
Science has its bangs and turns
But you will never end up having bad burns.

Stephanos Koutroumanidis
Orleans Park School

MY DOGS

My old dog Durky is now four
He lies around all day on the floor
He had no care, like a millionaire
But that's all changed now Saffey's there.

A spaniel black and white is she
A chessboard walking, young and free
She hassles Durk and makes him mad
They growl and fight, I'm sure Durk's sad.

Before he was the only one,
The only currant in the bun
But now he has to share it all
The food, the bed, the heater in the hall.

As Saffey grows Durk will learn
To be nice to her and wait his turn
But now they fight like cat and dog
Durk always wins, the heater hog.

Chelsea Brown (11)
Orleans Park School

WHO AM I?

Swiftly moving through the bushes
being as quiet as a mouse.
You would hate to have this creature
slithering around your house.

This creature is thin, but deadly.
His skin is scaly and also green
but this very deadly creature is
very rarely seen.

This creature's body is very long,
it can be at least as long as us.
But also this creature's body
can be as long as a bus.

But when this creature comes near you,
you think its fangs are fake,
but when he finally bites you -
you'll shout death to that *snake!*

Sam Riedlinger
Orleans Park School

THE STORM

It was raining,
Raining too hard.
The rain was like a football crowd
But louder.

As I watched the sea,
The sea watched me back.
When the wave broke onto the helpless sand
It pounded up the beach towards me,
But I was in my house,
The last safe haven in all this havoc.

Outside the trees swayed,
Like people at a pop concert.
The leaves fell off the tree
Like a melting ice cream.

My brain was jiggling
Like it was on a roller coaster,
I wish I was asleep
Not in this mindless
Whirlpool of chaos.

George Barnes (11)
Orleans Park School

MY CAT

My cat, he is as black as the night
and as cute as a puppy.
I rock him to sleep like a baby.
I call him he comes, only when hungry.
He gobbles his food then he hurries to the door
waiting to escape back into the night!

Ami Kitch (11)
Orleans Park School

CHRISTMAS

Christmas
time is here.
I run down
stairs and
into the living
room. It's early in
the morning, I've
woken Mum, Dad and my
little brother. There we
are, in front of the Christmas
tree, finding the presents
which are ours, ripping them
open. The wrapping paper's all
over the floor, what a mess. We go
upstairs and get ready, we're going to
see relatives.
Christmas,
what a
wonderful
holiday.

Emma Hastings (11)
Orleans Park School

FAST AND FURIOUS

Fast and furious
Yet calm and controlled.
Football is brilliant, so unforetold.
Any could happen, a goal or a foul
Or even a miss and a howl from the crowd.

Ben King (12)
Orleans Park School

NATURE

Nature! Nature!
The rustling leaves in the
Jungle restaurant, the breeze
blowing strong. Snakes slither
by, cheetahs chase their prey.
A pounce, a yell, gone. Lions
roar like the wind, monkeys
swing high into the
sky. Trees hang
over the
mud path
and the
dangling
vines.
Creepy-crawlies scatter by amongst the rotten leaves.
Nature!

Roxanne Bates (12)
Orleans Park School

THE GALE

The land was torn and twisted
its fertility torn from its hands;
a cruel thing is the storm
a plague upon the land.

On the eve of Christmas did it strike,
cutting through the silent night;
A legion of trees were first to fall,
despite their clutching to the ground, like
a mother would her baby.

Jamie Atkins (11)
Orleans Park School

FOOTPRINTS

In the winter
watch me go,
making footprints
in the snow.

In the spring
my boots are wet.
See how deep
the puddles get.

In the autumn
trees are brown.
I kick the leaves
all over town!

In the summer
by the sea
sandy footprints
made by me.

Chandni Babbar (11)
Orleans Park School

FOOTBALL

When you score the winning goal,
You're sure to be a hero
But if you miss a penalty
Your friends will go to zero.
If you're a striker
Then the pressure's on you
To score a great goal,
Better than anyone else can do!

Matthew Brandon (11)
Orleans Park School

My Cousin

My cousin is a mad monkey
He can never sit still
Although he tries
He bangs around like a hyena
And always hits the roof.

I like my cousin
Because he's nice to me
And gives me presents, when I'm down.
I bump my head
He's always there to help me out.

I always feel reassured with him
He never tells a lie.
We are the bestest buddies
Even if I only see him once a year
So hurry up and come to my house.

I like to play football
Or listen to music with him
We have fun on the PlayStation
Or just making a big loud din
We always have fun together.

Eleanor Batson (11)
Orleans Park School

Haiku

A little baby
Is so cuddly, cute and sweet
Like a little dog.

Melissa Patel
Orleans Park School

IMAGINATION IS THE KEY

Imagination is the key,
To unlock all your dreams.
It can be anything you want it to be.

It might lead you over the rainbow,
To that famous pot of gold.
It could take you to King Arthur
And those stories of old.

You might find yourself with King Henry VIII
From the exciting Tudor times
Or in the Amazon Jungle wrestling with a snake
Or beside a smelly witch who simply adores rhymes.

So as you can see,
Imagination is the key,
So keep on dreaming
And your life will be . . .
Well,
That's for you to decide.

Marina Hutchins Garcia (11)
Orleans Park School

PASTA

Pasta twirls,
Pasta curls,
Pasta shells,
Pasta comes in all shapes and sizes,
Pasta comes in many surprises.
Pasta is the best,
Pasta is above the rest.

Alex Juriansz (12)
Orleans Park School

THE RIVER

T
r
i
c
k
l
i
n
g
s
l
o
w
l
y
A
newborn
river gliding
over rocks
Gradually
Growing bigger now
Becomes a playful toddler
Meets up with some friends
Growing ever bigger, stronger
Now becomes a curious child
Playing with their friends
Running extremely fast
Just become a teenager
As rowdy as ever crashing into banks
A new set of friends vandalising everything
In their 20s now calming down not hitting banks
30s at its peak of speed going dangerously fast
40s now not as fast as before starting to age
50s now as slow as ever losing speed and strength
It stays like this for the rest of this long journey
Until it comes to a peaceful end in the massive graveyard
which is the sea

Liam Cooper-King (11)
Orleans Park School

MY FAMILY

My brother
Is a bother
His toys are
like his friends

He likes building
And constructing
Knocking over my things
Isn't very funny

My mum
Is wonderful
She's soft and cuddly too
If you need a
Shoulder to cry on
She'll be there
Just for you

My nan
Is Superman
In every kind of way
She won't ever throw
You away because
She's a super gran
Every step of the way.

My dad, Dave
Is totally wicked
With his super
Way every day.

Ashley Rollins (11)
Orleans Park School

THE OFFICE

An office rise, for the house of number five.
Suddenly there's a streak of light
coming from the desk.
The furniture is at it again.

The chairs are screeching down the office,
making footsteps in the dirty carpet covered in paper.
Making a glue floor for any human feet.
The furniture is at it again.

The computer is waiting like a lion,
Waiting for its prey.
The pencil is waddling like a penguin
not sure when he'll have a rest from the computer.
The furniture is at it again.

Suddenly the door opens,
There's chatter - where's the party?
The furniture isn't at it again!

Hanna Clarke (11)
Orleans Park School

WHAT COLOUR IS A RAINBOW ON MARS?

I have been asked many questions in my time
But never one quite as bizarre
As what colour is a rainbow which comes from
A planet called Mars?

I've been asked questions like
How many leaves on a tree? How long is some string?
And how many people will I ever see, to ask
What colour is a rainbow from Mars?

I thought for a while and then I decided
It's probably blue with pink stripes, purple spots, pink and fluffy
Turquoise, navy blue, red, yellow and black,
Green spots, white stars and orange.

I thought some more and then I decided that
There probably isn't a rainbow on Mars!

Ewan Henry (11)
Orleans Park School

OLD GRANDAD

Richard is his name,
Don't wear it out.
He's very grumpy
Very moody, but not very stout.

He has fake teeth
And calls them choppers!
It's hard for him to chew beef
And he's never been caught by the coppers!

My grandad calls me Smelly,
And always winds me up.
Whenever I watch telly
He always gets the hump.

Now when I play football,
He puts me to a test.
I know I'm better than him
But in real life, he's simply the *best!*

Steven Winter
Orleans Park School

MR SNAKE

This is a poem about Mr Snake
   Slippery, slimy, simple snake.
     Slithering as it makes ground
      As it bakes in the baking sun.

Hunting by day, also by night,
   Always wide awake!
     Whispering to its friends as it passes,
      Hunting! That's a piece of cake.

Mr Snake is a bar of soap,
   Slippery, like a water slide.
     Looking for shelter in deep, deep holes.
     Watching out for the moles.

Michael Hughes (12)
Orleans Park School

A CHEETAH

A cheetah is as fast as the speed of light,
The cheetah is the fastest animal in the world.
The cheetah climbs up trees and waits
for their prey to come and pass from under the tree.
Then the cheetah leaps down from on top of the tree,
and rips it apart.

The cheetah leaps across lorries, swiftly.
and silently, to cross the road.
The fur on a cheetah is as bright as the sun,
and it's as wild as a little boy.
The spots on a cheetah are as dark as the sky,
in the countryside.

Ivan Woloshak (11)
Orleans Park School

JAGUAR

A smooth rider
A cool walker
A mighty climber
Of dizzying heights

A silent slicker
As chilled-out as anything,
His glossy dark spots
Keep him camouflaged till night.

When at night
He comes out to play
A quick moving
Master of disguise.

A cool composure
An all-round ability,
To hunt
And kill.

King of the jungle
And a professional
Magician.
He could pop up anywhere.

Has a brain of a man,
Sharp teeth like a shark
You wouldn't want to meet him
In the dark.

Geraint Thomas (11)
Orleans Park School

ROARING THROUGH THE JUNGLE

Prowling, growling through the jungle
The green, ghastly, glaring jungle.
That's where I live
I jump on my prey, just for fun.

Being alert to every sound,
Learning to divert, to make
My prey lose track of me.
I tiptoe like a mouse through the night.

I buzz around the jungle, like a bee,
Stinging every ear with my roar.
I, the tiger, know everything.
Roar! I let everyone know I'm coming.

Eleanor Thompson (11)
Orleans Park School

MY SISTER MOLLY

My sister is a monkey, my sister
is a donkey.
She whines a lot, like a donkey
and acts like a monkey.
She likes to have a light fight
and a naughty one too.
When she's upstairs running
around the room.
Bang! Crash! Boom!
You can hear her all day long.
But you wonder what Molly is doing
and before you can blink, it starts again.
When it's bedtime, Molly is a kitten
sleeping on its bed.
Time flies by and it is morning again,
Crash! Bang! Bash!
She's running out of bed.
As Molly goes by, we both sigh
'Oh dear me, what a day to come!'

Jessica Cole (11)
Orleans Park School

MY AUNTY IS A PARROT

My aunty is a parrot
Or at least she looks like one
Her clothes are bright and fluffy
They make me sneeze and choke

She smothers me with kisses
With hugs, sweets and money
I don't mind the money part
But the hugs are not too much fun

My aunty is a parrot
Or at least she sounds like one
She always gossips to my mum
On and on about anything in sight

She always gives me presents
But not the kind you'd like
Daft dolls and daisies, even a drop of wine
And a Power Ranger doll from 1999!

Lily Beck
Orleans Park School

THE CAT

Cats are not all that they seem
They are as cuddly as a bunny
But not just that.

If you were to stay out until the
Darkest point of darkness
You'd see for real
Cats are thieves.

Cats are thieves because they
Slither through the night, and have
Midnight feasts of rotten kippers.

A cat is a midnight stalker
If you hear the cold air whisper
Behind you, beware - a cat is near!

A midnight stalker
Feasting, stealing
Ready to pounce, to kill.

Jodie McKnight (11)
Orleans Park School

THE ZOO'S MONKEY

The zoo's monkey, is an acrobat
Swinging from bar to bar.
But if it had a mile long pen
It couldn't get very far!

I think it's mean to keep it locked up,
In a tiny cage.
If the monkey was in a smaller enclosure
I would really rage!

The monkey is like a little clown,
Playing on a trapeze
But in the jungle, he swings on a vine
And of course, trees!

If I was a monkey in a zoo,
I would escape, wouldn't you?

Katherine Underhill (11)
Orleans Park School

MY UNCLE

My uncle, he's like a brick wall
He's got big muscles, he's very tall
He wanders about, but does not shout
My uncle, he's like a brick wall.

He's got a very grouchy voice
When he's asleep, he makes a noise
He comes out in the middle of the night
And that's when you get a fright.

Massimo Galletia (11)
Orleans Park School

TWISTER

The twister wraps itself around you like a set of chains,
It scoops you up off the ground, grinding you around
like a blender.
Cutting you into small pieces, no one can help,
They just sit and stare as it appears before them.
'Grab on tight!' they say. But it's no use, people
watch in their houses, wondering if it will stop.
They hear nothing, they hear nothing.
The family goes outside, they were never seen again!
Crash, bang, thump! The twister has
unleashed its victims!
They're puzzled as they lay hopeless on the ground.
Suddenly they hear something in the distance,
Could it be? No! Could it?

Jamie Elliott (11)
Orleans Park School

THE SEA

The sea, calm and swift
as people play in the
sand and the water.

Until night, the sea gushes
like herds of elephants, the thunder
smashing together like two saucepans.

The waves, big enough to drown five people,
and the rocks trembling as the water comes to
bash against them.

Then see the sun on the far horizon,
gazing across the sea, as day comes again.

Luan Austin-Duch (11)
Orleans Park School

I AM THE SAME AS YOU

People think they know *me*
Do you think they are right?
Always telling me to look for trouble
But I don't mean to burst your bubble
People are always telling me
To try my best and sue
So I'll be a walking millionaire
But I am the same as you.

So far in my life
I have told so many lies
But now I try my best
And not be a living pest
But it's just the way I am
I once *killed* a boy called Sam
But if you look deep down in me
I am the same as thee.

People think I am impolite
And they just walk away
It's not all my fault
That I don't know what to say
Children are so scared of me
And run away to their mummies
I'll give you a hint or two
I am just the same as you.

So when you now look at me
Don't you *dare* walk away
Once you get to know me
You'll be happy every day
But one little thing
Never mess with me
Or I can really hurt you
But I am the same as you.

But since I killed that boy called Sam
I now have learnt how to understand
I am as beautiful as the snow
Don't you know?
Now no one says to me
I really *hate* you
Because I think they now know that
I am the same as you!

Sabina Akhtar (12)
Preston Manor High School

FORESTS

Forests - safe habitat of millions of life forms
slowly being eaten away by axes and knives,
One by one, the creatures will fall,
never coming back.
Their coats and bodies are taken away
by the poacher's sacks.

If the animal numbers start falling, numbers of
tourists will start descending
The country will get poorer than ever
the poacher's money will start increasing.

Everyone's money will disappear soon and the
animals will be gone forever.

If we save the animals, they might just
end up saving us!
But if we kill the animals it will bring
more trouble and suffering.

David Ahn (14)
Preston Manor High School

CRIME AND VIOLENCE

My name is Lady Ree 4 u 2 nv
And I live in North Wembley.
Police in my estate every day
Also shooting in my alleyway.
Why don't the thugs stop?
Because their guns always go pop.
There's violence everywhere
But youngsters don't even care.
They must be fools
Because they want to act cool.
They can't even grow seeds,
They just want to smoke weed.
They want to have knives,
Don't care about their lives.
They want to have plots,
But they end up getting shot.

Reanne Sinclair (14)
Preston Manor High School

SUNNY DAYS

S   uper sunny days, all the time to play.
U   p and around,
N   ever sit down,
N   ever a dull and gloomy day,
Y   elping and yelling in the fields of green.

D   ays of joy, happiness and fun,
A   ll day we play, nothing is dull and grey, always fun and brightness,
Y   earning for more when night comes,
S   leeping the night peacefully away, knowing the sunny day is
     yet to come.

Christopher Sedze (13)
Preston Manor High School

UNTITLED

A lonely, isolated, forbidden house
Surrounded by a dark metal fence,
Shattered windows bolted by heavy iron bars,
Hence no sign of soul - life
Or expensive, modern cars.

No wonders of how its existence came about,
Nowhere to hear the screams or shouts.
Is that a whisper I hear,
A whisper through the air?

The wind whistles,
The bush leaves rustle
A whisper through the air.

The tree leaves shake,
And slowly flake
Into a heap on the cold ground
Which lies beneath.

Its location unknown to mankind,
Its mystery still to unwind . . .

Kinari Mehta (13)
Preston Manor High School

ROBOTS

R   un about with no life in them,
O   verloading with technology,
B   oosters on the backs of their metal bodies,
O   n full power,
T   ime to shut down,
S   hutting down.

Samir (13)
Preston Manor High School

My Friend's Death

I sat here on the bench
Waiting for my friend to come.
Soon she arrived,
Limping and looking glum.
When she sat down
I asked, 'What's with the limping?'
She froze then said
She fell down the stairs without thinking.

Throughout the whole day,
She acted really strange.
We wear tracksuits for PE,
But she didn't want to change.
When I put my hand on her shoulder,
She winced in pain and started to cry.
I knew what had happened
And if it were to continue she'd die.

She had four sisters
And two had already died.
She was told they'd died in a car crash
But she knew it was a lie.
When her dad got angry,
He would take his anger out on his daughters.
He killed his own wife
By drowning her underwater.

That night I told my dad,
'My friend's life is at stake.'
I wish I'd told him sooner
As when we got there
It was sadly too late.

Sabina Akhtar (13)
Preston Manor High School

VICTIM!

What do you see when you look at me?
A hyper guy or someone who is shy and sly.
I . . . am . . . the . . . same . . . as . . . you.

You bully me even when I'm at home,
I see an image of your disastrous face,
You think it looks good,
Obviously you would.
I . . . am . . the . . .same . . . as . . . you.

I'm at school 33 hours a week,
In most of the time I don't even speak.
Instead you taunt and tease,
I try to stay at ease,
You and your mates make it difficult,
I . . . am . . .the . . . same . . . as . . . you.

I'm not scared of you anymore,
I've seen your inner attributes you tore,
Just after you broke the school rules,
You are all just weak and fools,
I . . . am . . . the . . . same . . . as . . . you.

I have found my inner strength,
Now I can make you run the full length,
Now I have got many friends,
I know some of them are users,
But at least they are not like you,
The losers.
I am the same as you!

Harkaran Bajwa
Preston Manor High School

UNTITLED

A man boards a plane to go to a meeting in Washington,
little does he know that today will be a day the whole world stands still.
3 men with bombs and guns take over the plane,
they say we will all die, they give us a chance
to call our loved ones and say our farewells.
The man stretches out his hand to feel the painful pierce in his side,
he hears everyone screaming and falls into darkness.
The plane crashes into the World Trade Center,
Tower 1 followed by another plane into Tower 2.
Where is God on the 11th September?
Where are our allies?
Jesus kneels down to carve a heart in the sand
to remember and love those who died.
But out of all this, let us not forget the firefighters
who risked their lives for ours.
In a time like this, they are our heroes.

Teresa Hays (13)
Preston Manor High School

PAKISTAN AND INDIA

Why are there two countries fighting over some land?
These countries don't know they will wage war.
Both of them will be shattered into pieces,
Why don't they just stop and make peace?
The leaders don't realise what they're getting into,
Will they ever make peace?
They are crushing the whole world,
Come on *you guys,* make peace!

Bhavesh Patel (13)
Preston Manor High School

YOU'RE STILL A PERSON

I may be stupid, I may have done silly things,
I may be a hothead, I may have lost some friends,
I may be a victim, I may have been injured,
I may look different from many other people,
But I am the same as you!

You may have been stupid,
You were a victim of a crime,
You may have lost some friends,
You may look different from other people,
But you are the same as me!

You must look forward,
Don't dwell on the past,
Have a fresh start, you deserve it,
Come on because you are the same as me!

You are who you are
And who you are is you.

Because you are the same as all of us!

Dwayne Omaghomi (12)
Preston Manor High School

THE WORLD

The world is big,
The world is round,
The world is full of lots of sound.

The world is full of good,
The world is full of bad,
The world is full of sad.

Stephanie
Preston Manor High School

FRIENDSHIP

I have no friends at all
I am now all alone
I am worried
I don't know if I will make any friends
And I would like you to know that
I am the same as you!

I am a friendless person,
I would like to know why
I feel like I am getting weaker and weaker,
Every time I think about friendship,
I would like you to know that,
That I don't care what you think and
I will always be the same as you!

Is it my skin colour?
Is it what I am wearing?
Is it how I look?
What don't you like about me?
You should know by now that
I am the same as you!

I am kind and honest
I speak my mind
But I am still with no friends,
I wonder why?
I am the same as you!

I am proud of how I look,
I am proud of who I am,
I am innocent,
I have done nothing wrong,
But I still want you to know
I am and always will be the same as you
I am who I am.

There is nothing you can change
It is up to me what I do,
You don't have to tell me what to do
And for the last time
I am the same as you!

Sarah Hamoudi (12)
Preston Manor High School

THE SECRET WARRIOR

Her name is Sakura
Passionate and courageous,
A Japanese fighter
And very notorious.
Her fighting spirit fuels her confidence
And searches the world for a worthy opponent.

But one mystery warrior she is focused on
Is really smart and really strong.
His fighting style is better than hers
But she still fights on looking for him.

Sakura is eager to fight the warrior
And when she does she will be ready.
They have met only once,
But have never fought
But soon.
Sakura, the passionate fighter.

Jason Ellis Condison (13)
Preston Manor High School

ISOLATION

Why judge me by the colour of my skin?
This is how I have always been.
Treat me like you would want me to,
I am the same as you!

You have said enough things to me,
I have borne a lot, can't you see?
People like me aren't just a few,
I am the same as you!

You didn't say that to me before now,
I don't know why, I don't know how.
I might look different from you, may do,
I am the same as you!

You don't count the lessons that I've learned,
Nor the wisdom I have earned.
Look inside me, there is a person true,
I am the same as you!

I like myself exactly this way,
I don't value what you say.
I am incredibly beautiful,
I am the same as you!

Shikha Karki (13)
Preston Manor High School

SOLDIER

I'm a soldier,
I'm a soldier,
Even if my bones crush or crumble,
I will never fall or stumble.

I will never give up until
The judge lets me off,
Then I'll go home
And destroy the Millennium Dome.
I'm a man of war.

Rajan Aurora (13)
Preston Manor High School

THE FUTURE

What does the future hold?
Happiness or sadness, it begins to unfold
Will poverty cease?
Will Africa be rid of disease?
What does the future hold?
The story is being told,
Technology, inventions, pain and greed,
Will people learn to do more good deeds?
What will the future hold?
Will everybody's hearts become cold?
Will nuclear bombs be forgotten about?
Will countries be put out of drought?
What will the future hold?
Will mankind be more bold?
Will religion and race be accepted?
Will people's lives stop being affected?
What will the future hold?
Is life only money and gold?
Life can be held in our hands,
So mount it higher . . . like sand.
What can the future hold?

Davinia Champaneri (13)
Preston Manor High School

SCHOOL

School could be fun,
School could be boring
But the best thing about school is . . .
Lunchtime!
Lunchtime is wicked, I go to my secret hiding place
I look into a mirror, I see a palace,
It's got a rainbow over it.
It's as beautiful as a butterfly, I touch the mirror
Then suddenly
I'm standing on a marble floor, there's a spiral staircase
Going all the way up like a roller coaster.
There are rooms, over 1000.
It's a wonderful place, I would love to experience the adventure.
Suddenly I hear a bell and I find myself back in my lesson
I really can't wait till next time!

Sarah Hamoudi (13)
Preston Manor High School

FANTASY WORLD

An exciting adventure through your minds,
leave the wars, fear and anger behind.
Forget the changes that you fear,
and leave behind your tears.
Take a step into your mind,
reveal the fantasy inside.
Dreams you never thought would come true!
You'll be lent a hand and given a clue.
From then on, you're on your own,
Figure this journey out on your own.

Sana Rasoul (13)
Preston Manor High School

FRIENDS 4 LIFE

Friends 4 life is what we are,
Through thick and thin you were my friend,
Leaning on you, you gave me support,
The strength to get up and go again.

If my heart was shattered, you'd heal it,
If my heart was happy, we'd both rejoice in it.

You are my best friend,
Always and for ever,
It's been good,
The best friendship ever.
Never end, now and for ever!

Ayesha Patel (13)
Preston Manor High School

UNTITLED

I write this poem just for you
To make you think about my point of view.
Everything is not OK,
So, for example, I will say,
We should work and respect one another,
To bring out the best in us and each other,
Fairness and forgiveness should be granted,
To make us feel we are wanted.
Sadly my thoughts don't always count,
But if we work together, our duties won't mount!

Arti Bhundia (13)
Preston Manor High School

My Pet

I have a pet cat named Kitty,
She is so very pretty,
When I go to touch her fur,
Then she begins to purr
She is the best cat named Kitty.

When she comes in to eat,
I feed her some meat
And maybe some leftover beef.
She will never bite
Or get in a play fight
Because she's the best cat named Kitty.

When she needs love
I will give her a hug
Because I care
For her black, silk hair
So she must be the best cat named Kitty.

Paul Fergus (13)
Preston Manor High School

Raw

I want a snake,
I want to write a poem.
I want lots of things,
And know that I'm only dreaming,
Dreaming of having them.
I spent an hour thinking of a poem,
And now it's come to my head.
I have no pets, my life is boring,
A little excitement,
That's all I'm asking for.

My teacher gives me nothing to do,
She told me to sit next to someone,
I asked her who.
She then got angry, told me, *'Get outside!'*
All I want is to be happy,
That's all I'm asking for.
Just leave me this misery,
Just let me leave, open the door.
That is all I am asking for.

Mostafa Mohammed-Ali (13)
Preston Manor High School

SUMMER

I hear rabbits coming,
The first to stray,
Out of March
And into May.

And here comes a humming bird,
The first to fly,
Out by noon
And into the moon.

Here come the wasps,
Last to remember,
The end of September
And the first of November.

And here comes a lion,
The last to be dead,
Out of summer
And into bed.

Manisha P Bhudia (13)
Preston Manor High School

THE INTERNET

The Internet contains a lot of things,
From sport to games,
From education to entertainment,
There are sights for e-mail,
Like MSN Hotmail,
And sites for searching,
Like Lycos and Google.

The Internet is also very dangerous,
There are some that are anonymous,
And some that you may even know,
From talking in chat rooms,
To sending e-mails in computer rooms,
You'll have to be careful,
Very, very careful.

The Internet has a famous phrase,
Where is it @?
People answer with 'Blah, blah, blah dot com,'
Or with 'Blah, blah, blah dot co.uk.
All this causes confusion,
Especially with the elderly.

So the Internet is a confusing place,
Where people come to communicate,
Chat or research or play.
That is the Internet!

Nigel Ngo (13)
Preston Manor High School

SOULBLADE'S END

Soulblade, the legendary tale
It makes you fright
It will make you stale
It glows in the night
Like a fiery torch
And burns you up and makes you scorch.

Someone has to put this demon up hand
If anybody can do it you can
We need a warrior that has weapons
With might and magic it's you I reckon
With help with a friend to defeat this foe
Soulblade, a legendary tale.

Weapons slashing, fire flashing,
Attacks defence, dodges, blocking,
Is this demon unstoppable?
We need more heart and more passion
That will be enough to burn it out
The battle is over.

We have won the battle,
With feelings and faith
And swords and saucery,
Finally the nightmare is over
We did it with trust
For it is the end of
Soulblade, the legendary tale.

Jason Condison (13)
Preston Manor High School

REJECTED

There he was in the corner,
Standing there alone,
Thinking about what he could do,
All on his own,
Why his friends left him, he hadn't a clue,
He was going to say to them, 'I am the same as you.'

Just because he was fat,
His friends thought that he couldn't bat,
He got really annoyed at this,
Then he told this to his Miss,
She told him not to feel blue,
And she told him to say to his friends, 'I am the same as you.'

Every day he would come to school and say this phrase,
And his teacher and not his friends would give him praise,
He would often think about how he could play,
'Why you won't let me play. I haven't got a clue,
But until you realise that you have to judge me by the way I play,
But not the way I look,
I will always say,
I am the same as you.'

Now this boy is allowed to play,
Why he couldn't play before, his friends do not say,
He now feels very thrilled,
Now he doesn't feel blue,
And now he doesn't say, 'I am the same as you.'

Fahd Saleem (12)
Preston Manor High School

BURNT FACE

It all happened one day
I was walking down the street
This man saw me, he shouted at me,
'Ugly face,'
I got sad and angry,
I told him we are all the same,
It does not matter if my face looks like it's burnt.

Look at me, look at me,
I have got an ugly face,
I get sad by what that man told me,
From now on, I think about the future,
What I am gonna do with this ugly face,
Who's gonna marry me, but it does not matter,
Cos we are all the same.

It's been a while,
I got a job,
I have grown up,
My face is changed,
I am famous,
Everyone now likes me but
We are all the same.

I'm 24 now,
I know a lot,
I want to marry a girl,
She is pretty
I think I'm not good enough for her,
But she always tells me we are all the same.

Ehsan Salehi (12)
Preston Manor High School

I Am The Same As You

Different shapes and sizes,
Different coloured skin,
The inside is what matters
So to all those who are prejudiced
In the whole wide world,
Don't judge a book by its cover,
I am the same as you.

You are rare,
I am rare,
Life is rare,
So be proud of who you are,
All you need in life is yourself and pride,
Religion counts too,
I am the same as you.

In other countries all over the world,
Poor people starve,
While prejudiced people make fun of them,
We play computer games,
Think of the poor as you spend, spend and spend,
Send money to charity,
I am the same as you.

We think appearance is everything,
It is just how we look,
What people think doesn't matter,
They judge you from the outside,
What you say, what you do
Are the things that make you,
I am the same as you.

Mostafa Mohammed-Ali (12)
Preston Manor High School

NEVER WANTING TO WAKE UP

Every day when I go to sleep at night,
I say a quick little prayer and tell you to sleep tight.
Before I fall into my deep sleep I think again of you,
The one that I can't have,
But the one that I would love too.
The closest I can get to you is when you're in my dreams,
To know you and to touch you would be so surreal.

To look into your eyes
Is a mystery of the heart,
You have to search long and hard
Just to find your other half.
The one that you know
Will always be waiting for you
And the one that looks back the same way as you.

Your soul is covered so peaceful and deep
Your heart is whole so full and loved and sweet.
The little things you do could drive a person mad
The way you play with your hair
And the way I dream of you holding my hand.
So gentle and delicate
The way you hold a baby,
I would love to hear that you were my lady.

But all it is and will always be,
Is just a dream from a lonely stranger
Who will never be able to see your face so sweet
Unless they have to fall into a deep, deep sleep.

Binal Patel (15)
St Catherine's School, Twickenham

WHO I AM

I am the moon
and the stars in the sky.
I'm the words that you speak
and the tears that you cry.

I am the day
and the darkness of night.
I'm the rays of the sun
and the soft moonlight.

I am the ocean
and the rivers and streams.
I'm the precise realist
and the holder of dreams.

ı am the clouds
and the rain that falls.
I'm the purest of water
and the fierce fireball.

I am the desert
and the soft grains of sand.
I'm the driest of places
and the most barren of land.

I am the future
and the present and the past.
I'm the strongest sailboat,
built to last.

I am the soul
and the one who gives a damn.
So take a look at me,
for this is who I am.

Nadine Rajan (16)
St Catherine's School, Twickenham

JUST PASSING THROUGH
(For Nadine, Alex and Lisa)

I open my eyes and watch the sun, watch it rise and watch it set
I watch with friends, and those friends are you
But sometimes I find, despite all that it's easy to forget
In the eyes of the world, and the stars of the skies
I'm just passing through.

I remember, I remember the house where I was born
The portal door through which the sun, came peeping in at morn
It never came a wink too soon, or brought too long a day
The light we loved, the light we prayed would never go away.

My friends and I remember, the time when winter fell
The dreamy place, our fantasy world, where our hearts would dwell
Where flowers bloomed in summertime, where dew fell on the grass
Where memories dance in happy times, as shadows of the past.

And now my memory plays me false, as I slowly gaze at
The world we made,
The rain comes down, the candles dies and all the memories fade
And that is why we all wait here, alone and silent as the grave,
Thinking of the times gone by and all the peace and love we gave.

Don't bother yourselves, don't bother at all,
Does it matter to you, if we stand or we fall?
You know what they say, you know that it's true
In the abyss we call time, we're just passing through.

The four of us friends, we're just walking by
We carry no answers, and we can't tell you why
We'll make it somehow, our dreams will come true
Don't worry about us, we're just passing through.

Tamsin Austin (15)
St Catherine's School, Twickenham

THOSE DREAMS

When I woke up this morning from a dreamy sleep,
I wondered which dream was so deep,
Was it the one when I fell down a hole?
Or was it the one where I was chased by a troll?

Was it the dream when I travelled to the future?
Or was the dream when I discovered a funny creature?
Was it the dream when dad's started to fly?
Or was it the dream when I thought I might die?

Was it the dream when I met a talking dog?
Or was the dream when my prince was a frog?
Was it the dream when I was sitting in a cloud?
Or was it the dream which made me feel proud?

Still sitting in bed remembering my dreams,
When my curtain opens and the sun gleams,
There at my window two angels stand,
I close my eyes and they take my hand.

Out of the window and through the trees,
Here we go again for another one of those . . .

Dreams . . .

Bajel Patel (12)
St Catherine's School, Twickenham

LOVE

Did you ever love someone
And know they didn't love you?
Did you ever feel like crying
But what good would it do?
Did you ever dance with them
when the lights were low
And whisper, 'God I love him so,'
But didn't let them know?

Did you ever look into their eyes
And say a little prayer?
Did you ever look into their heart
And wish that you were there?
And so my friend, don't fall in love
You'll be hurt before it's true
Trust me my friend I should know
Because I fell in love with you.

Carly Byrne (15)
St Catherine's School, Twickenham

TO SOMEONE SPECIAL

You're someone special I know you are
The way you laugh and smile
The way you tell me not to worry
And stay with me all the while.

You're someone special I know you are
You make me laugh and cry
The way you shout and scream at me
But in the end I always know why.

You're someone special I know you are
I think about you all the time,
You support me through everything
To loose you would be a crime.

You're someone special I know you are
You drive me round the bend
You mean more than life itself
That's her - meet my best friend.

Lisa Widger (15)
St Catherine's School, Twickenham

OUR WORLD

In my life and millions of others,
We have experienced, war, pain and torture,
Many brothers, cousins, sisters and mothers,
Have been hurt because of this foolishness.

If we could all be friends
And live in peace
Our hearts could mend.

The creatures weep too,
For they can't live in peace and harmony,
They are slaughtered and tortured, just like us too.

The streets and the towns,
The city and the country are filled with fake smiles,
They are really crying inside,
I know how they feel, I feel too,
But I'm not afraid to show it on the outside.

So I ask you now, do you think
That two wrongs make a right?

Rochelle Mayner (12)
St Catherine's School, Twickenham

WAR AND PEACE

That tragic death-filled morning, when
Two mountains of brick laid down dead.
The loss of those you loved - the fear,
The devastation, the dread.
Innocent people leaving this earth and
Lonely children wandering the streets with
Their life shattered in front of them.
This is war: These are the effects.

A land of harmony
Where people of all races are united
Together as one,
Violence has stopped and love has taken over,
With free speech and justice for everyone,
This is peace. These are its effects.

Yasmin Raza (12)
St Catherine's School, Twickenham

ROWING ON THE RIVER

As I walk along the path
My heart starts to thump
I can't wait to get on the water
To row.

As I get into my boat
I start to glide across the water
My oar skims along the murky water
What lies at the bottom?
Who knows?

Branches float beside me
Ducks swim
I watch and stare
Taking every stroke with care.

When the wind blows against my cheek
I feel the excitement of whom I will meet
As my hand pulls my oar
I feel like I have pulled open a door.

There is a time
When you have to stop
To begin to row another day.

Imogen West (12)
St Catherine's School, Twickenham

MY WORST ENEMY

The angry, fat, ugly creature roared at me.
Its smelly breath was like a gust of wind blowing into my face.

I could see its hairy nostrils as it was so tall,
Its blood-shot eyes glared at me as I passed my lunch to it.

I watched as it ate my home-made cookies,
Its crumbs falling into my hair
Then it snatched my Ribena carton from my hand
And slurped it up in one big gulp.

It was the most hideous thing I had ever seen,
It had hairy legs and pointy big ears.
Its face was like a giant fierce animal
Almost equal to a troll.

When it had finished, it gave me my lunch box back
And stormed off to find something else to eat.

I sighed in relief as my friend comforted me.
I walked away and sat by myself, too scared to think
About the next day.

Annette Rowson (12)
St Catherine's School, Twickenham

TWIN WAVES

You look to nothing but blue glittering, shimmering sea.
The peace is broken by a white wave pausing for a moment . . .
The Twin Towers about to crash down.

Onto the shore of shells, the white
Towers crash killing thousands of
Innocent people!

Looking at the devastation in people's eyes,
It will never die.

The sea is calm once again,
It's still got little waves lapping at the sand.

Then out of the blue is a tiny albino dolphin,
Just a little shimmer, glimmer of hope that
Touches the hearts of many.

Genevieve Garside (13)
St Catherine's School, Twickenham

SUNSET AND MOONRISE OVER VALE DO LOBO

Evening.
Walk down to the shore and clear your lungs of the smoky town air.
Let the cool waves wash away the pain of the burning day from your
bare feet and then turn.

And see the radiant sun sinking, down behind the firefly lights of the
city, like some heavenly angel of hope returning to the ever-changing
clouds, turning the sea into a peach pool of tranquillity,
tie-dyed with dreamy oranges and pink water-colours, with the sky a
blaze of fiery glory.

And now, look to the east.
And you will see mother moon, angelic in her innocent pale glow,
rising over the cliff face where her side of the sky is soaked in dreams,
with a scattering of stars, a sleepy patchwork of soft lilac and midnight
blue. And stand there, solitary, staring up at the boundless heavens,
watching the moon rise and the sun set.

Walk home in the heavy darkness,
flitting through the moon shadows. Then stop on the clifftop and look
up at the starstrewn skies where the plough glints like chunks of
diamonds, the sea lit by the narrow slant of moonlight, as it is every
night and will be forever and ever and ever
Until the day the moon rises and the sun sets.

Caroline Gellatly (12)
St Catherine's School, Twickenham

UNTOLD MELODY OF LOVE

She weeps behind that door,
The one that screens her face,
For the love that was so strong,
Has been flung into a dark, horrible place.

He struggles in his blindness,
For his one true love,
She flutters all around him,
With the tranquillity of a dove.

Standing in silence,
Her heart does scream with sadness,
Painful thoughts are hidden,
By a face, written with gladness.

Standing in the centre,
The one who bears the crown,
He has conquered those,
Who tried to draw a frown.

The pearl of the ocean,
The most requested one of all,
She refuses to dance with anyone,
She is the princess of the ball.

A happy face does beam,
From the one who is alone,
He needs no one,
Just his friends and the place, that he calls home.

Together these people are bound,
Together as they shall rise,
Till around the corner it shall come,
Love, their perfect surprise.

Alice Hodgson (15)
St Catherine's School, Twickenham

SCHOOL FRIENDS

Pens and pencils all the same
Letters, words make a game,
Write a story, playing games,
Having fun all the same,
Make some friends and you will see
How important friends can be.

In the playground having fun,
When the bell goes, go in and
Study well and do your work
And you will get a good mark.

If you get to know the school,
You will see how important
Sunbury Manor can be!

Kayleigh Wright (11)
Sunbury Manor School

POEM

I saw a little pussy cat,
Lying in a ditch,
Sitting on a scrappy mat
And is scratching like it might have an itch.

As soon as I saw it,
With its sweet little eyes,
I had to keep it,
My parents said 'What if it dies?'

When I saw
Its little paw
And its tiny claw
We made a cat flap in the door.

Jamie David Robert Milton (12)
Sunbury Manor School

LIFTS

We got stuck in a lift
It shuddered a bit
Then went up a bit,
Then it didn't shift.
We shouted for help, nobody came
I turned white,
Oh what a fright!
We pressed the alarm,
Two men came.
They couldn't open the door,
I turned even whiter.
They tried again with a special tool,
It opened the door
So we got out alright.
I'm not going in there again.

Daniel Marenghi (11)
Sunbury Manor School

GOING OUT WITH MY MATES

I like to hang about with my mates,
We have a giggle and a laugh,
We hang about at the park,
We sit on the swings,
Talking about things,
Till my mobile phone rings,
Off I go homeward bound,
Going to listen to the latest sound.

Leanne Coward (12)
Sunbury Manor School

ANGELS OF THE WATER

The waters lap onto the sand,
The sun has set behind the land,
The waves are skipping above the sea,
I can hear the angels calling me,
Their happy whistles, their graceful moves,
They're swimming, jumping above the blues,
They're diving deep beneath the waves,
Hiding in the watery caves.
I'm walking on the water with the dolphins beside me,
I'm flying like a bird above all that I see,
The water laps onto the sand,
The sun is rising above the land,
The waves are skipping above the sea,
The angels of the water have left me,
Then I wake, it was all just a dream,
But why was it more real that it seemed?

Gemma Richards (14)
Sunbury Manor School

OLIVER THE CAT

Oliver is a very old cat,
He's big, round, plump and fat.

He sleeps all day, comes out at night,
This often gives us a terrible fright.

Hissing and spitting all night long,
Then he comes home with a great yawn.

His favourite food is fish and chicken,
When he's finished he keeps on lickin'.

Sarah Ayton Sharpe (12)
Sunbury Manor School

FOOTBALL

Football is my game,
Craig is my name,
Brentford are the team,
The players are so keen.

Chelsea are the best
They do a lot then rest,
The players are fantastic
Because they are enthusiastic.

It's normally a 4-4-2
They work hard for you
90 minutes is full-time
And also the end of my rhyme.

Craig Hiskett (12)
Sunbury Manor School

NETBALL

Watch them as they hit the ground
And then see them turn around.
As they jump to get the ball,
Watch out, you might have a fall.
Then the ball goes up the pitch
And you don't have time to even have an itch.
Then the ball is passed along
And the umpire watches to see if anything goes wrong.
Then the netball is in front of the post,
Then it goes in, oh no, almost.
It's a goal by goal attack.

Stacey Searle (11)
Sunbury Manor School

DAYDREAMING

My elbows on the table,
My book in front of my face,
I close my eyes and daydream
I escape to another place.

A place of fun and laughter,
A world that never cries,
No tears or endless shootings,
No bombings and no lies.

A day with light and joking,
A smile to each one's face,
A place of peace and dancing,
But it's only an imaginary place!

Charlotte Stewart (12)
Sunbury Manor School

THE STORM!

The lightning is flashing,
The thunder is growling,
The rain comes down crashing,
The stormy wind is howling.

The cloud will never clear,
The storm will carry on,
The sun will never appear,
The lightning hasn't gone.

The sky has now turned blue,
The clouds are now not grey,
Now I can do what I wanted to do,
I'm going outside to play.

Radhika Tankaria (12)
Sunbury Manor School

AMERICA'S WAR ON TERRORISM

There's no money
There's no possession,
There's only George Bush
And his war on terrorism.

First it was bin Laden,
But did he go unscathed,
Iraq's now in the firing line
War's path already laid,
Britain backs the US
Again we're by their side,
Now to persuade the UN,
To help us turn the tide.

There's no money,
There's no possession,
There's only George Bush
And his war on terrorism.

With or without the UN,
George Bush will carry on,
Determined as we know he is,
To keep the war on terror strong.
There's nowhere you can hide Saddam,
Your regime will crumble
Your evil ways will meet their end
And you'll be defeated and humbled.

There's no money,
There's no possession,
There's only George Bush
And his war on terrorism.

Shane Smith (14)
Sunbury Manor School

A SKI HOLIDAY

The mountains stretch high,
The Pistes run low
And everything sparkles,
With soft, white snow.

The rays of the sun,
Shine through the air,
As you climb the mountain,
In a lift chair.

Crisp, white snow,
Wind on your face,
This is the feeling,
Of a ski race.

The flags mark the way
The whistle blows
And like the saying,
'Away she goes.'

The mountain's trees,
The wooden chalets,
All of these things,
Make a perfect holiday.

A week has gone,
It went so fast,
Before we knew it,
It was in the past.

The mountains stretch high,
The Pistes run low
And everything sparkles
With soft, white snow.

Elaine McNamara (14)
Sunbury Manor School

MY LIFE

I am a young child
How life has been hell,
My mum and dad don't know me so well,
Since I was six, I've been living in a home,
This life has been as hard as stone.

At the age of six and a half I moved home,
I didn't like the surroundings, I felt all alone,
The house was to big, lots of people came around,
I got scared, I fell to the ground.

At the age of nine, I was settled in my new surroundings,
I started to like lots of people around,
It seems so bad, but it improves,
So no longer do I have the blues.

At the age of twelve I felt like one of the family,
We went on holiday and had great fun,
It's starting to feel like I've got a real mum.

At the age of fourteen, I have realised that life is too short,
I put into practice what I have been taught,
Soon I'll start the search for a suitable lad,
I won't let my children have the start I had.

Natalie Lockyer (14)
Sunbury Manor School

FISHING ON A SUNNY DAY

Relaxing on a sunny day,
Hoping the fish are going to bite away.
Watching the calm water, as it swivels around and around.
I lie my rod upon the ground.

I see my bait, which the fish is to take.
I strike my rod and it starts to break.
I realised I had a really big bite
Alas, the fish swam off into the night!

Michael John Beecham (11)
Sunbury Manor School

THE ENDLESS JOURNEY

His birthplace, a mountain cloaked in white,
A glimmer of sunshine at the ice did bite.
Forever friendly, a playful child,
Innocent and oblivious to the dangerous wild.
Creamy froth parties with a foamy rush,
Whilst on the banks the roses blush.
As fish flit on to various places,
A flurry of bubbles brightens patient faces.
Spreading his roots and yearning to broaden,
A kingfisher looks on like a watchful warden.
No enemies lest the bitter cold wind,
Who makes ripples echo and calm waters spin.
He befriends all he can, no judgement he carries,
At vicious spiked forks with twins he marries.
Softly meandering along an unknown passage,
Then gaining strength, becoming savage.
Stubborn and wanting to get his way,
The dirty sides crumble, relentless they decay.
A small jolt of movement awakens shadowy depths,
Strongly and forcefully is the sediment swept.
A mumble, a rumble, a sliver, a shiver,
Gently, yet powerful, is the ever-changing river.

Laura Jessett (14)
Sunbury Manor School

ROUNDERS

You grab the bat and wait for it to come,
You hit the ball and then you run,
Round the posts you go,
Running fast, not slow,
I wait and wait and then I'm called,
I grab the bat and watch the ball.

The ball is thrown 1, 2, 3.
I hit the ball with flying speed,
I can't waste time I have to run.
If I make it then we've won,
I'm sprinting, I'm sweating from the heat.
I'm running so hard it's hurting my feet.
7, 8, 9, 10.
Yes, I've made it to the end,
The posts I've run round, 1, 2, 3, 4,
Oh brill' I've made it what a score!
Great! I've reached the end,
Finally I've done it with my friends,
'Let's all cheer, hip, hip, hooray!'
I will always remember this day!

Daniel Walsh (11)
Sunbury Manor School

FIFTEEN SIGNING IN

Number 1's called Wally,
Number 2's called Tub,
Number 3's called Thicko,
4's always down the pub!

Number 5's quite fast,
6 don't take a seat,
Number 7's very small
And 8 he likes to eat.

Number 9 is good at night
And number 10 is Tuff
Number 11 failed his exam
All subs bite their nails.

This is all my rugby team
We are a funny bunch
After we win all our games
We look forward to the lunch.

Sam Wisden (12)
Sunbury Manor School

FAIRGROUND POEM

A day at the fairground is always fun,
People are talking, some people are walking,
Some people like the tea cups that whirl around,
Others the spooky ghost train that goes underground,
Sounds of fear coming from the right,
People being thrown from quite a height.
The old Carousel people don't want any more,
They find it a bit of a bore.
Carts from the roller coaster whizzing past,
Some may think it's going a bit fast,
Dodgems always a laugh crashing into each other,
There's such a big queue, they might want to build another
People having a laugh and a joke,
Whilst sipping their can of Coke,
Flashing lights from the Ferris wheel,
What a day I can reveal.
I can't wait another year
Until the fair is next here.

Simon Yewer (12)
Sunbury Manor School

FOOTBALL IS?

Football is a crazy sport,
They dribble round and round,
The lazy keeper could have caught
The ball that hit the ground.

Football is very well supported,
They shoot from every side,
The best of players are rewarded,
They shoot with skill and pride.

Football is played with a ball,
Arsenal keep on trying,
Chelsea of course can beat them all,
Leeds's population dying.

Football is made up of teams,
Teams keep on competing,
World cups made up of dreams,
They keep the heart on beating.

Stephen Curtis (12)
Sunbury Manor School

HAPPINESS

Happiness is yellow, the bright
Colour shining like the sun,
Happiness is a horse prancing
Around a field and having fun.

Happiness is watching the sun,
Set upon the beach,
Happiness is sharing your
Sweets just one each.

Happiness is a waterfall crashing
To the ground,
Happiness is a fox chasing its
Tail, running round and round.

Happiness is not being sad,
Happiness is being very glad.

Michelle Brown (12)
Sunbury Manor School

A KATZ LIFE

As I wake from my sleep,
I must remember to keep,
My claws from scratching,
At the sofa where I was hatching,
A plot to catch my next meal.

As I stretch my limbs,
I suddenly spot the Pimms,
Although I really oughta,
Be sticking to my water.

Now it's time to eat,
I'll climb onto my feet,
Now scratch at this foot,
Until my meal is put,
Down in front of me, what strife
This purrfect idea of a cat's life.

Simon James Osborne (13)
Sunbury Manor School

FOOTBALL

I want to play for Man United
Because they are really good
They have good players
I really wish I could.

My favourite player is Beckham
I think he's really cool
He plays in right midfield
And I think he rules.

Van Nistolrooy is class
His nationality is Dutch
He plays at centre forward
And he's got a good first touch.

Roy Keane is our captain
Our driving force
He has a bad temper
Then gets sent off of course.

I hope you liked my poem
I think it's really good
I hope you think the same way
I really wish you could.

Scott Rowan (12)
Sunbury Manor School

TILL DEATH DO WE PART

As you walk faster, he does too,
You can't look back, he's following you.
You can't run on, he might have a gun,
He's stalking you down, this just isn't fun.

He's covered by shadows,
The street lights are dim,
By turning a corner,
You still can't lose him.

He's getting closer,
His breathing is deep,
Hands in his pockets,
You're starting to freak.

Slowly and calm,
His grasp becomes firm,
He lifts his hands from his pocket,
You know this will hurt.

You take your last breath, your sins you admit,
As he pulls on the trigger, your body goes limp,
This is the gun, that took your life,
And these are the tears, we still cry every night.

Mariesha Phipps (14)
Sunbury Manor School

LIFE'S AUCTION

What good are we
If we can't find the key to the door,
That leads us to so much more?

Going once . . .

What chance do we have,
If ignorance is the way,
Gradually we'll pay.

Going twice . . .

It's no scientific fact
We're going to have to make a pact
For the compassion we lack.

Going, going . . .

So take a step back and reconsider,
Must you always be
The highest bidder?

Gone.

Samantha Oakley (15)
Sunbury Manor School

MY JOURNEY

I get up in the morning
And go to the station,
Is the train late?
I'm going to lose my patience.

Once the train is here,
It is all crammed pack,
I fight for a seat,
But I haven't got the knack.

Speeding along the track,
Through the dark tunnels,
Some people are sleeping,
While the children are blowing bubbles.

I'm finally at the station,
Case in my hand,
Show the man my ticket,
Off to work I ran.

Nick Munday (12)
Sunbury Manor School

FREE

I wish I was a bird flying high,
surrounded by the moonlit sky,
up there not a care in the world,
the clouds overlapping and curled.

So free, so alive, an open door,
to go inside and explore,
a road so long you could go
to heaven and back,
a long trail too deserted to track.

But listen to me carefully,
'cause I can see
what lies ahead for us all,
even if you are tiny or tall.

What lies ahead you should not fear,
or even shed a tiny tear
'cause God will be there to hold your hand,
and look after you the way He looks after His land.

Joanna Eden (12)
Sunbury Manor School

THE BIG ONE

I walked up to The Big One
The music playing really loud
I didn't know if I would go on it
But I knew if I did
My mum would be really proud.

As I got closer in the queue
My heart started beating faster
Would I get too scared?
But then I saw the headmaster.

It looked like he was scared
As it was going really fast
And then when he got off
It didn't look like he would last.

As I sat down in my seat
Then it hit me
I was so scared
I thought I needed a wee.

I span round and round
Not even moving in my seat
And then the ride stopped moving
And I couldn't feel my feet.

I thought the ride was wicked
And now I'm not even scared
I wonder if my friends would go on it
But it's probably something
They wouldn't be able to bear.

Cindy Stevenson (12)
Sunbury Manor School

HORSE RIDING

Go horse riding on Friday,
£8.50 I pay.
Get a ride in the school bus,
Bump, bump.
We never make a fuss.
We arrive before Miss Kay.
All the horses go *nay, nay.*
Teacher asks us to lead rein,
But 'No thanks' I say.
Go and get my stuff,
It can be quite tough.
Northie's on the board,
My favourite horse of all.
I can't wait to get on,
The lesson won't last long.
I'm riding round and round,
Queen of the paddock, I should get a crown.
Oh no, the tractor's in the yard,
This might come to be hard.
Aargh! He got spooked.
I could see his feet,
My heart and throat meet.
He never used to be like that,
He never used to be so fat.
So now the lesson's over, I feel the colour of clover.
But now I can go home,
I'm tired, I hope it hasn't shown.

Emma Rogers (12)
Sunbury Manor School

IMAGINE

Imagine falling flat on your face,
  before the day has had its grace.
Imagine having thundery weather,
  before the day has had its pleasure.
Imagine the sky full of sun,
  when the day has just begun.
Imagine if we had order in everything we do,
  nothing would be fun or playful for you.
Imagine nothing sweeter than honey,
  except people's stupid money.
Imagine the day we have today,
  to lie about and to play.
Imagine having no play,
  just a boring old day.
Imagine if poems never had a rhyme,
  nothing would be in time.

Constance Burse-Treagust (13)
Sunbury Manor School

SHOPPING

I went on a shopping spree to see what I could buy,
There were only socks and my horrible underwear.
There were no good CDs out, just old men's ones.
So I decided to go and buy some buns for me and my tum.
I ate my buns which were yummy, yummy.
I looked at the clock, saw that it was 6 o'clock.
So I decided to go home to watch telly,
Then go to bed to dream about jelly.

Daisy Lucas (11)
Sunbury Manor School

SCHOOL DAY

You wake at seven,
The sky is grey,
On goes your uniform,
It's another school day!

You wait outside,
The bus is late,
You get to school,
Just as they close the gate.

The dog ate your homework,
Detention again,
Your friends all desert you,
It's all pain, no gain!

You get to lunch late,
All the food's gone,
Extra homework,
Your bag weighs a ton!

Lost your bus fare,
You'll have to borrow,
It's not all that bad, but . . .
Do I have to do it again tomorrow?

Natasha Halliday (12)
Sunbury Manor School

NOW AND LATER

I like football
I like swimming
Not long before I like women.

Chris Barnett (12)
Sunbury Manor School

147

WHY?

Why is the sky blue?
Why do cows say 'Moo'?
Is the grass greener on the other side?
Or perhaps it's as blue as the great blue tide.
Why does it rain and why is there pain?
Why do we talk and why do we walk?

Why does the world speak differently?
Why does the world always puzzle me?
Why do questions make you wonder?
What's most frightening . . . lightning or thunder?
Why does everyone eat and drink?
Why does everything make you think?
And why do people have to die?
Why do I keep on asking why?

Claudia Srodzinski (11)
Sunbury Manor School

RESOLUTION

Egg, bacon, salt and pepper
The ingredients to have to get a bit fatter.
Chocolate, crisps and fizzy drinks
The worst things to have when you're on a diet.
Don't you think?
One, two or maybe three burgers at once.
A large chips and apple pie to munch.
Then off to the gym to lose those pounds,
The ones you gained when you were down.
From ten to twenty stone in under a year
All you are is a failure to the New Year.

Luke Channon (15)
The Matthew Arnold School

MY SCHOOL DAY ROUTINE!

My alarm goes off and I have a cough.
I'm leaping down the stairs half asleep,
Ready to jump in my chair for breakfast.
I clean my teeth and wash my face
Whilst looking like a zombie.
I'm getting dressed in my school uniform once again.
As I go to brush my hair, I look like a bear with messy hair.
I catch the bus without a fuss.
I go to tutor on a scooter,
A girl in my tutor blew her hooter.
I munch my lunch with a crunch.
At the end of the day
I like to remember what I did last may.
I listen to my music instead of losing it with my brother.

Kerry Hopkins (15)
The Matthew Arnold School

CHRISTMAS POEM

The children playing in the snow,
Shouting, screaming *Ho! Ho! Ho!*
Santa is watching, Santa is watching,
Be good or nothing in your stocking.
The sun comes out in the morning,
The snow begins to thaw
And the frost is there no more.
The children are happy, to
See what else is in store.

Danielle Hill (11)
The Matthew Arnold School

SPIDER

The spider crept on his bed
Cold shiver went down his spine.
The man jumped out of his bed, and scared
The spider wiggled away.
The man went to get a broom
The man fetched a broom as fast as he could.

Sidney Spider on the wall
Sidney Spider had a fall
He called and called but nobody came
And he lay there all day long.
He started to sing a song,
All of a sudden along his friends came.

Spider, spider over there
Spider, spider everywhere.
Oh dear my fly has flown away,
Spider has been flown away
Oh I wish it could be May
Make it change to a beautiful day.

Spider, spider has no hair
Spider, spider, no one cares.
Family and friends still love me the same way
Other animals don't care.
Oh why do they stop and stare.
The sun reflects on my bald head every day.

Max Hathaway (12)
The Matthew Arnold School

HALLOWE'EN!

Hallowe'en, Hallowe'en
No more sparkling teeth with a gleam.
The time to have fun and dress up,
Give me some sweets and fill a cup!
Trick or treaters at your door
Whatever you do don't ignore!
Everyone goes to parties
Don't forget to give me Smarties!

Hallowe'en, Hallowe'en,
It's a good time to be seen.
Trick or treaters with make-up
All over your face,
Clean it off later just in case,
There is no bit of heat
So come on then give me a treat!

Hallowe'en, Hallowe'en
A time when monsters will be seen.
All pumpkins light up the room
When the mummy creeps out of the tomb.
All the witches wearing their hats
Look all around, there're flying bats.
In come the creeping cats
Not forgetting all the rats!

Lydia Mazzone (11)
The Matthew Arnold School

A Lonely Night

It's dark, what shall I do?
I can see no light coming through.
Can't see my book,
Can't see the clock.
All I can hear is *tick, tick, tock*.
Shadows jumping. Why?
I don't know,
They're getting closer,
Watch them grow.
What's that noise?
I've not heard that before.
Maybe an owl, maybe a bat!
Or could it be a ghastly rat?
The wind is blowing, I can hear it howling.
The leaves are rustling and the creatures come.
The clouds come over and we have a shower.
I sit there and watch.
My fear washes away.
I drift to sleep as I say I had such a happy day.

Jessica Chadwick (12)
The Matthew Arnold School

The Tramp

I'm out of my nut on one pound seventy-four.
A bottle of cider is always fine.
Walking the streets is the worst of time
But down on my luck I never find a dime.

But down in the subs is Christmas for me
I always find something to please me.
With pennies and pounds I'm happy as can be
I'm out of my nut on one pound seventy-nine p.

Daniel Roche (16)
The Matthew Arnold School

YOU!

You!
Your head is like the moon.
You!
Your eyes are like diamonds in the night.
You!
Your ears are like clouds.
You!
Your nostril is like a squashed star.
You!
Your mouth is like a spaceship.
You!
Your hands are like the world.
You!
Your belly is like the sun.
You!
Your legs are like basketball bats.
You!
Your backside is like a crater.
You!

Rosie Martin (12)
The Matthew Arnold School

THERE'S A DRAGON

A dragon went to market, to see what he could find,
but people thought he was a toy, so he
flyed, flyed, flyed.

The next stop was a farm, to see what he could find,
the farmer thought he was a monster, so he
flyed, flyed, flyed.

The dragon stopped at a library, to see what he could find,
but he was too noisy, so he
flyed, flyed, flyed.

He went back home to his cave, to see what he could find,
but there was his dinner, bath and bed, 'cause he was
tired, tired, tired.

Kathryn Griffin (15)
The Matthew Arnold School

PENSIONER'S PLIGHT

Each day they wake and Arthur Itis comes to stay
He knows he's not welcome but he comes anyway.

He goes to the shops and on walks with them,
They meet their friends they all know Arthur Itis.

But he doesn't stop them having fun.
Maybe one day he will go away.

As hard as he tries to stop them in his tracks
General Practitioner tries harder to mend the cracks.

Adam Howes (12)
The Matthew Arnold School

THE DAY YOU SAID GOODBYE

When you said you were going I felt like crying.
It felt like my heart was slowly dying.
I used to dream of us being together
I used to dream that we would be forever.
I never dreamt it would end like this
Don't you realise it's you I would miss.
Before you came I didn't know what to do
But that all changed when my eyes fixed on you.
My heart beats faster when you walk through the door
And take my hand and lead me to the floor.
When we danced and you span me around
It felt like my feet were leaving the ground
When you took me in your arms and held me tight
I felt like I was flying just like a kite.
Now you are going nothing will be the same
My heart won't beat faster when they call your name.
It's hard to imagine you will be there no more
I'll wish for the day you walk through that door.
So goodbye is all I have left to say
So have fun and I'll see you again some day.

Victoria Elford (16)
The Matthew Arnold School

IT IS . . .

It is as tall as three giraffes on top of each other.
It is as round as the sun.
It is as shiny as stars at midnight.
It is in the most wonderful place, England.
It is in the most busy city, London.
Can you guess what it is?
It is the London Eye.

Cheryl Loveridge (12)
The Matthew Arnold School

WINTERTIME

Colder and colder
Means only one thing
Wintertime is coming.
The snow falls on the ground
Covering the ground in a
Soft, white blanket of snow.
Out to play come the children,
Snowball fight, snowman building.
Jack Frost is out to play
The children run indoors
And cuddle up by the nice warm fire.

David Sims (11)
The Matthew Arnold School

FRIENDSHIP

F   riendship,
R   emember those days?
I   t's like it was only yesterday.
E   nd of friendship will never come,
N   ever breaks up between two best friends,
D   reams are for sharing with friends,
S   un rising between us two,
H   appiness rising upon us two,
I   will always be there for you
P   ast we will never forget.

Iqra Shafique (13)
Villiers High School

FOXES, BADGERS AND RABBITS

Foxes, badgers and rabbits,
All lived by canals,
Until the pollution came along with litter,
Then half the animals had to leave their homes
And others died,
We have to stop this pollution,
For the animals,
Please stop the pollution and put the litter where it belongs,
Not in the animals' homes,
So *stop* all the pollution and the litter,
Because it's destroying the animals' homes.
Stop!

Ruby Khella (12)
Villiers High School

MY DOG IS CALLED ROXY

My dog is called Roxy
And she is very large.
Her eyes are like footballs
And her stomach a garage.
I played with her yesterday
And probably will today.
She makes a lot of mess,
But I love her more than my favourite dress!

Nitu Ahluwalia (12)
Villiers High School

THE MORAL

Tell the world what you are
Tell them what you can do
Give the best of yours
Create a world of your own,
Always learn from your mistakes.

Take the gift of knowledge.

Be attractive as a flower,
Be hard as a diamond.
Also think of studying,
But don't forget to play,
Try to always rise,
But if you fall
Don't lose confidence,
Try and try and you will be successful.
Respect your elders,
Because they are gold,
Respect your teachers,
Because they have a role.
Respect everybody.

Respect yourself.

Try to be calm,
Experienced and not harm,
Just try to learn
The things taught,
Experience the experience.

That's all I want to say,
But remember them to follow
And if you can't
Then try and try till the goal is achieved!

Anand Shankar (12)
Villiers High School

THE STRESS OF EXAMS

Today I live,
Tomorrow I shall die,
I do not know what to do,
Except to cry.

Exams are near,
I did not revise,
I have to come clear,
I cannot tell lies.

My heart is pounding,
What can I do?
I am in trouble,
Please give me a clue.

The exam day has arrived,
I have done nothing at all,
Here I am now,
Sitting quietly in the hall.

Teachers are stressed,
While their pupils are in pain,
'Write good information and good explanations.'
These are the words spiralling in my brain.

The exams are over,
I'm back to my old routine,
I'm waiting for my results again,
Worried, if you know what I mean.

Rina Bhinder (12)
Villiers High School

MOTHER

Mothers are always there,
Mothers always have signs of good luck,
Mothers know what's happening,
Mothers are clever people.

A mother's love is big, even when you die,
Mothers' hearts are huge,
Mothers' love never ends,
Mother I love you.

Mothers are things that you will never dream,
Mothers never leave without love,
Mothers' love is so great for you,
Mother I appreciate it.

What will children do without mothers?
We all thank mothers
And the extra love received,
Thank you so much.

Sonia Zafar (13)
Villiers High School

MUM'S LOVE

Mum is someone who loves you.
Mum is someone who takes care of you.
She is someone who shows you love
And gives you all of her heart.
She never disowns you no matter what.
Mums never show you the wrong way,
They always show you the correct way to go.

Jessica Jackson (13)
Villiers High School

THE BURNING TOWERS

She lay amidst the dust,
Choking on the dry blood clogged in her throat.
Within her quivering arms
She held the steaming corpse of her dead daughter.

Tears burned as they ran down her face,
Just as the ferocious fire had burned,
The once soft, gentle skin of her daughter.

The smell of burning flesh penetrated her lungs,
As cancer engulfs the body.
She lifted her hand to wipe away the constant flow of tears,
Leaving a streak of blood on her high, taut cheekbones.

She ceased to weep and acknowledged the deadly silence,
Anger surged through her pumping veins.
Her heart pounded and sweat dripped onto the burnt corpse.
She then let out a desperate scream,
'Why Rosalia?'

Penelope D'Acquisto (17)
Vyners School

A NOTE

This is just a note saying
I won't be coming back.

I can't take it anymore;
The meat stinks,
The customers moan,
I've missed my break
So now I'm going home.

Anthony Bremner (16)
Vyners School

THE GREAT LOSS

Life goes on into the deepest friendships,
Until you've gone and you can never mend it.
Now it seems like it was a dream,
But how long ago you will never know.
Look what you've done you've broken so many hearts,
Now what's become of all the people that were torn apart?
And all your promises broken,
All your words left unspoken.
All those people that you've upset,
Now what can they do?
They can't just forget.
It was you that helped them survive,
And you that kept them alive.
It was you that created the main atmosphere,
You that they knew were always near.
But now that you are no longer here,
Your place in their hearts will always be dear.
For it was you that made them happy
And you that made them glad,
It was you that made them cry
And you that made them sad.
You that brought them happiness
And you that brought them grief,
But now that you're no longer around
They'll have to turn over a new leaf.

Nisha Mehta (17)
Vyners School

SEASONS

Spring is when the grey days cease
The herald of unending peace
Spring is when the bluebirds fly
Winter's days extinguish and die
Spring is the time for new beginnings
Watch out when fortune's wheel starts spinning

Summer is the time Apollo shines
A mixture of fruit drinks of lemon and lime
Summer is when the horizon is endless
The priceless beauty that leaves us speechless
Summer is heat, and glory, and blaze
A timeless season among hazy days

Autumn is the golden touch of Midas
The warm with the cold, deep inside us
Autumn is the time for the turning of the leaves
A change in the air; in the life our souls breathe
Autumn represents the setting sun
The last glimmering ray, before winter comes

Winter is the start of long dark days
A mysterious season; a riddle or a maze
Winter is the time for cool black nights
When it's easy to feel the cold's icy bite
Winter is also the time for celebration
The wishes and hopes of a hundred nations.

Lyndsay Glanfield (17)
Vyners School

TEENAGE DESIRE

Let me eat your eyes
So I can see just what you see.
Let me wear your ears
So I can hear just what you hear.
I'll peel off your skin
So I can feel what you feel.

You're so pure
I want to be you
You're so perfect
I want to be you

Feed me with your wit
Let me drink your intelligence
Let my eyes feast upon your beauty
I want to devour your soul
I want to swallow your ideas
And bring them up as mine.

You're so innocent,
I want to be you,
You're so naïve,
I want to be you.

I'll face your fears for you,
I'll lift your burdens for you,
I'll scare your demons for you,
So they don't trouble you,

Can I touch your heart?
Can I linger in your mind?
Is my name on the tip of your tongue?
I want to be you.

Katie Sawyer (17)
Vyners School

IF

If only I had stayed in bed,
If only I hadn't got up,
If only I had spoken out more,
If only I had just shut up.

If only I'd gone on a diet,
If I'd learnt to live with my weight,
If only I'd planned for the future,
If only I'd accepted my fate.

If only I'd done what the grown-ups had said,
If I'd challenged authority more,
If I'd learnt to feel less deeply,
If I'd cared just a little bit more.

If only I'd learnt to grow old,
If only I'd acted my age,
If only I'd stayed where I knew I was loved,
If only I'd flown from my cage.

If I'd told my parents I loved them,
If I had just let my children go,
If sometimes I had just said yes,
If only I had learnt to say no.

If only I didn't look back with regrets,
If only I wasn't so smug,
If only I could have more time on Earth,
If only they'd pull out the plug.

Hannah Crowley (17)
Vyners School

TWO YOUNG GIRLS

Two young girls vanished like thin air
Several thousand people showed that they cared
Dressed in matching outfits
Going out for a walk
In their own town having a talk.

Their phones turned off, nowhere to be seen,
Security cameras didn't show where they'd been.
Days went by without any news
Their parents just sat there, silent and bemused.

A few weeks later they were found lying there
With TV screens on, all people could do was stare.
Two young lives taken on a whim
Never to see their beloved families again.

Why do people do such hurtful things?
To reflect their lives an angel sings.
Families torn apart from losing their young
It's all over now nothing can be done.

People were questioned, neighbours and all
The police sat and waited for the all important call.
As we sit and wait for the trials to begin
The light at the end of the tunnel is so very dim.

Cheryl Wood (17)
Vyners School

STOLEN FUTURES

One day so innocent,
The next, just gone.
Futures are stolen,
Lives aren't so long.
So much sorrow is felt
And tears are cried,
For the young lives lost,
Happiness denied.
Grief unites us all,
We feel the pain.
For families and friends,
It's an endless strain.
Living in constant fear,
Is it safe to play?
Not trusting anyone,
Or what they say.
Will justice be served?
We start to ask.
This can't be forgotten,
Memories last.
This terrible heartache,
A growing trend
And still it continues,
When will it end?

Susanne Morgan (17)
Vyners School

DE PROFUNDIS CLAMAVAI: (A PRAYER TO THE WORLD)

I hear your voice,
your promises trapped in the circle of the past,
shadows covering the centre present,
yet another twisted monster
de profundis clamavai: a prayer to the world.

The stench of your vengeance,
forces in the air bring decay,
the fall is coming,
can you hear the screaming,
de profundis clamavai: a prayer to the world.

Your hungry eyes waiting for the demise,
a white world of brimstone,
the blood in your eyes,
you, the human blasphemy,
de profundis clamavai: a prayer to the world.

Matthew Jukes (17)
Vyners School

DEAR MISS, A NOTE TO SAY ABOUT WHAT HAPPENED TO MY HOMEWORK . . .

Dear Miss,

I'm glad to say my essay's done,
I finished it yesterday,
I've got it right here in his bag,
But what can I say?

My cat chewed up my essay,
She spat on it too,
So now my essay's ripped to shreds,
But what can I do?

There isn't much to see,
But I brought it anyway,
I'm going to put it on your desk,
I hope I get an 'A'.

Iqvinder Malhi (16)
Vyners School

MY INSATIABLE LOVE

Ivory black, smooth as velvet,
Encased in a silver wrapper.
Textured as silk,
Soft golden toffee and crispy chunks,
I crave another!

I like white, milk and oh so dark,
From exotic lands and shops aplenty,
From an admirer, friend, or from my own pocket,
A chocolate existence is my desire.

It doesn't matter how many rolls I gain,
Or how many buttons burst.
I like chocolate cake, chocolate mousse and chocolate pieces,
And then a chocolate dessert!

And if someone said . . . there was no more chocolate,
If the world came crashing down,
I think I'd have to go to Heaven
To live in my very own chocolate town!

Sarah Saunders (17)
Vyners School

MILLIE DOWLER

Six months had passed,
Body found at last.
Hope is buried
Relief in your place.

Thirteen, too young to die
Six months, too long now knowing.
Your fragile bones is all that was found,
In a woodland, near Hampshire,
By mushroom-filled grounds.

At least now your parents will know,
Never to expect you home.
Cause of death, still not known
Sorry you had to die alone.

Wishful thinking seems now a waste
As you were destroyed with such haste.
Your death will have justice someday, somehow.
Rest in peace Milly Dowler for now.

Charlotte House (16)
Vyners School

DREAMS

The girl I see before me,
all so withered and pale,
she wants it all,
so full of ambition.

Her ambition is trapped,
forced to travel the path,
all so misty and dark.
Why not pick the warm inviting path?

Doomed by powerful monsters,
deafened by the screams of,
'Choose my lonely and miserable path.'
Just don't remember your dream!

Natalie Totham (16)
Vyners School

STAIRWAY TO HEAVEN

Deep in a sleep, I'm falling, falling deeper
But I'm wide awake, opened, opened are my eyes
Vivid senses, I've never felt before regained
From another existence that inexplicably I know.

Mauve; as deep as the endless maze of velvet
                    curtains that surrounds this nirvana.
White mint green as crystalline as my first morning.
Birdsong trickles like heavenly water in a sunless sky.
Little cerise lights drop like spinning stars
A rainbow wraps around me like satin and lifts me higher.
My skin; covered in diamonds of every colour,
The deepest aquas and brightest reds,
Of golden leaves and lilac mist.
An azure stillness shoots in ripples from me.
Stillness surrounds the soft murmur of the willow
As deep evening purple exhales between each leaf.
I descended in slow motion
Floating amongst the stars
As my heart fell at the speed of light.

Lyka Kinchen (16)
Vyners School

THIS IS JUST TO SAY

This is just to say
I'm sorry

I wish
I had never treated you the way I have
I realise now that I was wrong

I know
That there's probably not a lot
I can do to take away the hurt

I want to
Make it up to you but I'm guessing
This time I've gone too far

But this is just to say
I'm sorry.

Stephanie Dixon (16)
Vyners School

MY POEM

Yesterday I tried
The best I could
To write
A poem
That would rhyme

And also
That would make sense
As I'm not a good poet

So now it's complete
Read it
If you please.

Jonathan Haynes (16)
Vyners School

AROUND THE ROOM

Looking around the room
you try to judge whom
is the biggest, the best person.
You, me . . . them?

Doubting yourself
means you're vulnerable.
Inadequate feelings felt,
fool.

Forget status.
No one's better than you
and you're no better than them.

New ages, people, places
means uncertainties.
Not knowing when to do, what to say.
Who's his and hers?
Who's history?

And where do you fit in?
Being the youngest
with the most to say?

Emma Harrington (17)
Vyners School